WAITING FOR GOD

Trusting Daily in God's Plan and Pace

Xochitl Dixon

Our Daily Bread
Publishing™

Requests for permission to quote from this book should be directed to: Permissions Department, Our Daily Bread Publishing, PO Box 3566, Grand Rapids, MI 49501, or contact us by email at permissionsdept@odb.org.

Author is represented by the literary agency of Credo Communications, LLC, Grand Rapids, Michigan, credocommunications.net.

Scripture quotations, unless otherwise indicated, are taken from the Holy Bible, *New International Version*®, *NIV*®. Copyright © 1973, 1978, 1984, 2011 by Biblica, Inc.™ Used by permission of Zondervan. All rights reserved worldwide. zondervan.com.

Scripture quotations marked cev are from the *Contemporary English Version*. Copyright © 1991, 1992, 1995 by American Bible Society. Used by permission.

Scripture quotations marked nlt are taken from the Holy Bible, *New Living Translation*, copyright ©1996, 2004, 2015 by Tyndale House Foundation. Used by permission of Tyndale House Publishers, Inc., Carol Stream, Illinois 60188. All rights reserved.

Interior design by Beth Shagene

Library of Congress Cataloging-in-Publication Data
Names: Dixon, Xochitl, author.
Title: Waiting for God : trusting daily in God's plan and pace / Xochitl Dixon.
Description: Grand Rapids : Discovery House, 2019.
Identifiers: LCCN 2019018313 | ISBN 978-1-62707-973-0 (pbk.)
Subjects: LCSH: Expectation (Psychology)—Religious aspects—Christianity—Prayers and devotions. | Waiting (Philosophy)—Prayers and devotions. | Trust in God—Christianity—Prayers and devotions.
Classification: LCC BV4647.E93 D59 2019 | DDC 248.4—dc23
LC record available at https://lccn.loc.gov/2019018313

Printed in the United States of America

20 21 22 23 24 25 26 / 8 7 6 5 4 3 2

Contents

Hope for Long Days

You are not alone. That's not always easy to remember, especially when we're going through difficult days that stretch into months, maybe even years. When the wait feels endless, the frustration is real and the weariness can overwhelm at times. I've tasted the bitterness of hopelessness. *How long do I have to wait, God?*

But I've also savored the sweetness of the Lord's unchanging goodness and loving faithfulness as He showed me that patience has nothing to do with waiting for Him.

Whatever we're going through, we can cry out to God and trust that our words are not falling on deaf ears. Even when it seems like God is silent, He is at work. He is with us. He loves us. Our all-knowing and all-powerful God hasn't forgotten His promises. And He'll never forget us, leave us, or let us go.

He'll never forget you, leave you, or let you go.

God is working in ways you may not understand right now, but He's waiting for you. Yes. He patiently extends His grace as He calls us to draw nearer to Him, to listen for His voice, to simply rest in His limitless love. In His silence, He calls us to be still so we can experience His might and His mercy. So He can empower us to trust Him fully. One day, one step, one breath at a time.

Our faith may falter while we wait. We may doubt our ability to take one more step or wait one more second. But the Lord remains with us . . . carrying us through, holding us when we don't have the strength to hold on to His promises. And He sends others to support us, others who understand the all-too-common faith-droughts that drain the confidence from our strides as we drag through the desert.

As I began to understand the loving interdependence of the body of Christ, waiting became an act of worship. I rejoiced as I witnessed the Lord working in and through my life and the lives of those around me. Together, we could rely on Jesus, rising *and* resting in victory. We could thrive in the peace of His constant presence, wrapped in the security of simply being His beloved children. Together, we could trust His sovereign goodness and flawless planning.

While writing this book, I experienced the soul-penetrating power of testimonies. Each person's story strengthened my own faith, rooted my hope deeper, and brought me life-giving joy and life-affirming peace. And that's my prayer for you.

As we walk together through the next 31 days, I pray that your faith will be strengthened. Each day we'll look at an eternal truth based on God's Word. Then you'll be prompted to read a passage of Scripture. Please don't skip that step—God talking to us through His Word is the best way for us to understand His purposes as we learn to accept and be transformed by His perfect and unconditional love. After we see what God has to say in His Word, we'll witness the power of His provision through the wait. We'll take a look at the testimonies of His people and discover applicable truths from our Scripture reading. Each chapter includes questions for reflection that can be used for small group discussions. I'll be inviting readers to join me on my blog to discuss those questions, too. You can become a part of my blog family at xedixon.com and also connect with me on Facebook, Instagram, and Twitter. I'd love to come alongside you so we can encourage one another on this exciting journey.

I pray that each living testimony will give you hope for the long days. That you'll find assurance that God can be trusted and that He is truly good. That you'll be able to bring each closing prayer before the Lord with confidence. Together, we will *inhale* the truth of Scripture, *exhale* prayers of honesty and belief, and find *rest* in God's enduring love . . . all while we're still waiting and trusting daily in His plan and pace.

1

The Weight of Waiting

TODAY'S TRUTH

*God's Word secures us in hope
as He does the heavy lifting during the wait.*

TODAY'S READING: *Psalm 119:73–90*

I knelt at my recliner in the dark living room, overwhelmed with increasing back pain and frustrated over another setback in my healing journey. Once again, muscle spasms that had begun in my upper back spread to my shoulders and neck, causing a debilitating headache. For hours I suffered, overcome with nausea and desperate for crackers so I could take medication. I didn't want to burden my son, Xavier, while he worked. And my husband, Alan, was at a business meeting hundreds of miles away. I sobbed with loneliness and hopelessness.

As stabbing pain shot up my back and neck and my head throbbed, I texted a friend and asked for help. Within thirty minutes, two sisters in Christ arrived with boxes of saltines. They sat with me, prayed with me, and cried with me.

Finally able to nibble on crackers, I took medication and curled in a fetal position on the sofa. I sniffed as tears slid down my cheeks and onto my pillowcase. I waited . . . and waited . . . and waited, to no avail. *How long, Lord? I can't stand it anymore. Please . . . take me home.*

My prayer shocked and scared me. I asked for forgiveness and started praying for others I knew who were stuck in their own whirlpools of waiting. I thought about the brave Christ-followers in my life. Faithful believers who placed their hope in God, waiting wearily and expectantly. People who praised God equally through heartbreaking sorrow and contagious joy. The details of our different circumstances didn't matter as much as the focus of our faith—Jesus. Through intercessory prayer, I proclaimed God's bigness was enough for my friends.

So, why would I doubt He was enough to carry *me* through?

I kept right on praying, right on reaffirming what I knew to be true even when it didn't feel true, right on worshipping the Lord with tears . . . until I fell asleep.

My friends stayed with me until Xavier got home from work. When he arrived, our loving friends bombarded him with advice on how to care for me.

My twenty-one-year-old's voice, deep and matured beyond his years, pierced my heart. "I know how to take care of my mom," he said. "She's been sick my whole life."

His whole life?

I thought I'd done a good job managing motherhood and my pain before my body gave out on me in 2012. My hoping-for-healing wait had impacted my son and my husband more than I realized. *How much longer do I have to deal with this, Lord? How much longer do they have to suffer?*

After my body recovered from the flare-up, I prayerfully searched for comfort, peace, and hope in the Psalms.

Who am I kidding? I wanted to whine with the best of the pity-party psalmists. I wanted to feel better about being weak. I needed assurance that my hopelessness could be understood. I read psalm after psalm, longing for affirmation that my waiting . . . and waiting . . . and waiting on God wasn't in vain.

Then He led me to a verse right smack in the middle of Psalm 119:

> In your unfailing love preserve my life, that I may obey the statutes of your mouth. (v. 88)

I definitely needed a life preserver, though I had no idea how obedience to God's Word would keep me from sinking into despair during impatience-producing pain. I read on:

> Your word, LORD, is eternal; it stands firm in the heavens. Your faithfulness continues through all generations; you established the earth, and it endures. Your laws endure to this day, for all things serve you. If your law had not been *my delight*, I would have perished in my affliction. I will never forget *your precepts*, for *by them* you have preserved my life. (vv. 89–93, emphasis mine)

As I read each verse over again, the Lord shifted my attention from my weakness to *His* limitless might displayed in the vastness of the heavens. God's majesty and eternal faithfulness surpasses suffering and encompasses suffering. The Lord's enduring promises trump hopelessness. Though the emotional and physical weight of waiting while dealing with affliction often seems endless, God and His Word are everlasting. Calmness flowed deep as I closed my stinging eyes and reflected on the psalmist's words. No matter how much time passed, my Lord is and always will be the eternal maker and sustainer of the universe. Scripture reveals God's sovereign goodness and grandness. Because I could trust His unchanging Word, I could follow His lead with confidence.

Whether we're waiting for a trial to end or a dream to be fulfilled, a burden to be lifted or hard work to be rewarded, the Ruler of time itself remains trustworthy. Slow progress—or no progress—can cause us to bow down under the heaviness of discouragement. Physically, mentally, emotionally. But through His Word, where we encounter His unchanging character and incomparable promises, we can find peace.

As we weigh His promises against the worries of this world, God can erase our doubts and lift the seemingly unbearable weight of waiting.

INHALE

Your word, O LORD, is eternal;
it stands firm in the heavens.
—PSALM 119:89

EXHALE

Lord, our hearts can feel so heavy from the weight of waiting. Please have mercy on us when we're weary and weak. Hear our cries as we plead for your healing hand to cover us, as we long for you to deliver us, restore us, renew us, and redeem us.

Forgive us when we obsessively desire anything more than we want you.

We know you are compassionate, Lord. Still, the wait can often feel overwhelming, the pain or the longing can feel too much to endure. We can begin to wonder if you'll have compassion on us. Please forgive our doubt. Help us persevere in faith as you carry us through our current situations. Help us depend on you for all our needs, while waiting for deliverance. Help us to hang on to everything your Word teaches about who you are.

Come, Lord. Save us because of your unchanging goodness. Save us according to your perfect promises. Stay true to your infallible Word and save us, Father, because of your unfailing, life-transforming love. Help us trust you, even when we're bowed down under the weight of our seemingly endless waiting seasons.

In Jesus's name, Amen.

- How does remembering that God's Word is eternal help us trust Him when our wait feels endless?

- Return to Psalm 119 and read verses 92–93. How can delighting in God's law preserve our lives and keep us from perishing in our affliction?

- Which verses from the Bible help you focus on God's power, love, and faithfulness instead of on the burdens in your personal walk through the wait?

Lord, help us trust that your unfailing love
will carry us through all circumstances.

2

It's Not All about Me

TODAY'S TRUTH

*God weaves every detour and delay into His
all-encompassing plan for all His people.*

TODAY'S READING: *Genesis 45:1–11*

After praying for spiritual growth, it was painful to learn that my aggravation with waiting stemmed from my toe-tapping impatience and self-centered pride—traits that almost destroyed some of my closest relationships, including my marriage. While God patiently worked on my heart, I stubbornly dug in my heels. I insisted I'd be happier if He would just change other people. After all, *I* wasn't the problem.

Life would be grand if my husband would just realize *his* need for growth. The time would pass much smoother if my friends and coworkers would recognize *their* issues and if my estranged family members would finally take responsibility for *their* parts in our conflicts. Why should I be merciful in forgiveness over and over again? Why did I have to be the one who chose to be patient in love, waiting and waiting and waiting for others to be more like Jesus?

During an über-long season of pouting and complaining about how much my husband needed to grow, God gently nudged me toward a deeper study of the life of Joseph. I'd been whining and waiting for my husband to grow spiritually instead of asking God to mold *me* through the wait, so I could reflect His image in and through my relationships.

I'd like to say I immediately started surrendering to the Lord and that I embraced change. But I can't. The more I considered the possibility of inviting God to do a life-transforming work in my heart, the more I trembled at the time commitment.

I didn't mind the stretch marks of spiritual growth, but the thought of slow progression drove me berserk. And how could I possibly focus on my own growing pains when everyone around me seemed to refuse accountability?

It took me a while to discover the answer I'd evaded for years. If God knows me completely, hems me in behind and before, and is always with me, I could trust He didn't need my help watching the clock or trying to handle—okay . . . *control*—everyone else's life.

If I could believe God keeps His word, I could rely on this truth to be applicable across the board. I could act like I remember life is not all about me. God loves *all* of His children and understands *all* our struggles, our character flaws, and our desperate need for time and opportunities to help us grow.

As we deal with our anxious thoughts and humble ourselves before our King, we can count on Him to remain with us and lead us through the paths He's paved for us. He's the one who secures our confidence in His goodness and love. He is even the one who enables us to trust His ability to carry us, to hold us up, and to make us new. As we invite Him to complete His life-transforming work, we can cry out, "Change me, Lord! And help me stop trying to change everyone else."

Unfortunately, heart-deep change requires time and sometimes includes a bit of humbling through suffering and affliction. Joseph's wait—intentional and vital for his leadership preparation—helped him learn how to acknowledge God's grander vision and purpose, even when bad things happened to him. His journey started in his own home with his dysfunctional family

(Genesis 37–50). As a teenager, Joseph was favored by his father, and so his brothers envied him. In hatred, they faked Joseph's death and sold him into slavery. While he served as a slave in Egypt, as if that wasn't enough, he was wrongly imprisoned for two years. During all of that hardship, the Lord remained with Joseph and made him prosper. Ultimately, God restored Joseph's reputation and brought him back into a place of respected leadership. His wait, riddled with adversity and God's abounding grace, refined Joseph's character.

The names he gave his sons are testimonies of Joseph's acceptance of God's purposed detours and delays in his faith journey. Through his first son's name, Manasseh, Joseph proclaimed that God had made him forget all his trouble (Genesis 41:51). When he named his second son Ephraim, Joseph said, "It is because God has made me fruitful in the land of my suffering" (v. 52).

Though famine spread through the whole country after the birth of his children, Joseph seemed to have left his past behind him and rose with confidence in his leadership position. Just when things seemed to be going his way, Joseph's brothers showed up looking for help and didn't even recognize him. He took time to process his feelings, keeping his identity a secret from his brothers until he could no longer control his mixed emotions. His siblings had no clue God had been doing a major heart-overhaul during his trial-filled waiting season, and they feared retaliation.

Joseph made it clear that he hadn't forgotten the rough roads he'd traveled or the danger and devastation he endured because of his brothers' betrayal. But he realized how God deliberately intertwined his life with the lives of others. Instead of lashing out in anger, Joseph comforted his brothers and said, "Do not be distressed and do not be angry with yourselves for selling me here, because it was to save lives that God sent me ahead of you" (Genesis 45:5). Instead of harboring bitterness, Joseph accepted God's hand in the good and the bad. Instead of being bound by unforgiveness, Joseph extended mercy and promised to care for his family. This great leader understood that every moment of his journey was being used to bring glory to God's name and deliverance to his people.

Joseph's story affirms that God's sovereignty and power cannot be thwarted by the actions or attitudes of the people He created. Even those who deliberately hurt us do not control the outcome of any difficult situation that may come our way. As God's interdependent church (made up of all the believers in Jesus), our lives impact the lives of others. Our waiting seasons affect us but also other folks, some of whom we may not even know. Though we'd like to believe the world revolves around us, God reminds us that the world He created and sustains revolves around Him and Him alone.

When the journey feels impossible or way too long, God gives us all we need to trek up the twisting trails of the Meantime Mountains. As the Lord prepares and refines us according to His purposes, He is also preparing and refining others whom His plan will impact. What happens to *us* is never just about *us* as individuals. When we focus on living for God, like Joseph, we can accept everything that occurs during the wait as an opportunity to grow closer to Him and others.

INHALE

The Lord is trustworthy
in all he promises
and faithful in all he does.
—PSALM 145:13

EXHALE

Lord Almighty, Creator and Sustainer of all, thanks for assuring us that you are all-knowing, all-good, all-loving, and always in control. Thanks for reminding us that every second we spend in the valley of waiting has great purpose in the refinement of our character. Please help us settle into the roles you've designed us to play in your perfectly ordained plan.

Thanks for helping us realize the value of connection and communication, both with you and with others.

As we face difficult situations, detours, or delays, please deepen our trust in your faithfulness. Help us to accept your refining process.

Use relational conflicts to make us more like you and help us live like we believe the wait is not all about us.

In Jesus's name, Amen.

- How can considering how closely our lives are intertwined with the lives of others help change our perspective regarding trials and the time we spend in the wait?

- Why is it often tempting to ask God to change others quickly instead of focusing on the ways we need to change and accepting the time required to make those changes stick?

- How has the Lord used the time you've spent in the wait to help prepare you for something you never expected?

All-Knowing God,
thanks for working in all of our lives,
individually and collectively,
through the wait.

3

Holy Vision

TODAY'S TRUTH

*Holy vision helps us see beyond our wants
and trust God's will in the wait.*

TODAY'S READING: *1 Samuel 1–2*

Dreaming. Praying. Waiting. Hoping. This ongoing cycle is an adventure bursting with opportunities to witness God's mighty and merciful hand leaving prints of faithfulness on every aspect of our lives. But when waiting starts to exhaust us, it's easy for our vision to narrow. Doubt, insecurity, fear, and impatience can trickle into our minds and prick at our guarded, but tender, hearts. Can we really reach those dreams? Does God truly hear our prayers? How long do we have to wait before discouragement snuffs out every last bit of our hope?

When we're struggling to hold on to an inkling of faith, we often ask the Lord to strengthen us. One way He answers this prayer is by shifting our gaze away from the mirror. As we look beyond our own concerns, we see God at work in and through the lives of others in the Bible and in the world around us. Our field of vision widens, and our faith deepens as we're reminded that our limitless God reaches farther than the boundaries of our personal space.

Witnessing the ways God works in the lives of others strengthens our assurance of His ability to work intimately in our lives.

If He can work miracles in the lives of others, He can certainly work miracles in our lives and handle our puny, non-miracle-requiring needs. Right?

Unfortunately, that confident faith can get a bit shaky when our wait slips from days into weeks, then months, then those all-too-often hope-snuffing years. What happens when our faith is stretched, seemingly to its breaking point? What about when we reach for those dreams and fail? What happens when we see our prayers answered in such a way that it changes what we're waiting for and diminishes our confidence?

After doctors told my friend Diane Dokko Kim that her son was cognitively disabled, she admitted to becoming "spiritually crippled." The dreams she had for her son were gone forever. He would never be able to experience the life she desired for him. She struggled with overwhelming fear. Guilt battered her weary soul. She battled feelings of inadequacy when faced with her redefined role as a parent of a child with special needs. She sobbed through night after night of processing prayers: Why my son? Why me? What will happen to him without me?

Emotional turmoil can prune our tender hearts and transform tight-fisted prayers to open-palmed cries for mercy. Wrapped in the grace of God, Diane and her husband loosened their grip on their picture of a perfect life for their son. They depended on the Lord for the power to take one step at a time and trust one breath at a time; and He helped them sift through the ashes of their dreams to discover the beauty of rekindled hope. Diane now shares her story while wearing a Savior-Dependent Survival Badge. Encouraging others by assuring them that they're not alone, she proves day by day that waiting on God is worthwhile. In her book, *Unbroken Faith*, she affirms that hope is plentiful in the refuge of God's relentless love and faithfulness.

Diane's beautiful redemption story reminds me of Hannah's bittersweet surrender that led to one of the most remarkable demonstrations of selflessness in Scripture. Hannah was one of

Elkanah's two wives. The Bible tells us, "Peninnah had children, but Hannah had none" (1 Samuel 1:2). Tormented by years of Peninnah's cruel mocking, Hannah wept bitterly and begged God to open her womb. In her longing for a child, she failed to appreciate the love her husband poured over her and didn't even seem to acknowledge the love God had for her. She pleaded with the Lord and made promises from the depths of her desperation. Facing ridicule and false accusations, Hannah prayed with fierce faith until the local priest, Eli, blessed her, giving her confidence that God would answer her prayers. Though thrust into another season of wandering in the wait, Hannah's perspective had changed. Now believing that God would open her womb, she accepted His timing as perfect and, when she gave birth to Samuel, proclaimed Him as the God who answers prayers.

From the tone of her prayer in 1 Samuel 2:1–10, it seems as if Hannah was able to keep her grip loose in a show of loving trust. It seems evident that Hannah worshipped the Lord, her Rock, while waiting with expectation, knowing she would have to give up the precious child she'd been dreaming of for years. But as she prayed after surrendering Samuel, Hannah revealed her deepest desire was to please the God who heard her, answered her prayer, and prepared her to walk through the wait with faith secured in His proven faithfulness.

With renewed hope strengthened through the gift of holy vision, Hannah learned that freedom of love, in her case, meant to have her son, not to hold him forever. It seems that she was able to acknowledge Samuel was ultimately God's beloved child, a child with a purpose greater than what she was able to see, a child the Lord loved more than she could even begin to fathom. After she placed Samuel into God's hands, she bore five more children. With an unselfish love, Hannah marched on, offering support from the sidelines, as Samuel fulfilled his purpose in God's greater plan.

Hannah's life is a beacon of hope that still inspires selfless surrender. When pleasing God overrides our desires to demand our way, we develop holy vision. With holy vision, we too can proclaim the Lord is trustworthy as we place our lives, and the lives of those we love, into His care forever.

INHALE

There is no one holy like the LORD;
there is no one besides you;
there is no Rock like our God.
—1 SAMUEL 2:2

EXHALE

Mighty and merciful Creator and Sustainer of all, thank you for assuring us that we are never out of your reach as you give intimate attention to the details in our lives.

With Hannah, our hearts rejoice in you. There is no one holy like you; there is no rock like you. Mold us to better reflect your character. Help us trust you're working out your perfect plan in spite of the trials occurring in our lives and in the lives of those we love. Rekindle our hope, faithful Father

Thanks for allowing us to feel, for encouraging us to come before you with raw emotions without fear of condemnation. When our motives become self-centered, please loosen our grip on our own desires and align our hearts with yours.

As we wait on you to move, please help us look beyond ourselves. Help us to wait with fists unclenched and arms wide open to receive your always-sufficient grace and provision.

Father, we know that it is because of your sovereign goodness and love for every child in your interdependent church that you do not give in to our selfish grumbling, and we thank you for that. Develop our holy vision so that we will want to please you above anything else.

In Jesus's name, Amen.

- How does focusing on the holiness of God increase our depth of trust in His motives and mercy?

- What aspects of God's character affirm His reliability and feed our hope through the twists and turns we'll encounter in the wait?

- What is God asking you to release your grip on this week?

We love you and need you,
our ever-present, ever-powerful,
ever-purposeful Lord and Savior.

4

Just Say the Word

TODAY'S TRUTH

When the wait feels endless,
we can practice taking God at His Word.

TODAY'S READING: *Luke 7:1–10*

Words can linger long past the moment each syllable is breathed into existence. With the power to wound, bind, build up, and tear down, our words can become weapons of destruction or healing balms of deliverance. We can use words to confuse, persuade, discourage, comfort, guide, manipulate, and encourage. Positive words often require repetition to break through the scarred walls of wounded hearts, while negative words often appear to have the sticking power of superglue. The Bible affirms the power of our words: "The soothing tongue is a tree of life, but a perverse tongue crushes the spirit" (Proverbs 15:4). Clearly, words can have a lasting effect on the heart of the hearer. So much so that Scripture urges us to recognize and take responsibility for the power of our speech by taming our tongues (James 3:1–12).

My courageous young sister in Christ and YouTube personality Emma Mae Jenkins understands the scarring pain of careless words. She also realizes the great potential of using grace-laced words to extend compassion as she influences others to place their trust and hope in the Lord. As I served as her writing coach, God used her to change my perspective on how I allowed negative words to influence me. With contagious joy and bold faith, Emma remains committed to inspiring others to celebrate our God-ordained uniqueness as she speaks His infallible and timeless words of truth with love and authority.

Sadly, her journey has been long and hard as cyberbullies attack her character, her family's integrity, and her physical appearance. The ongoing abuse often cuts deep, wears her down, and tempts her to believe the lies that lead to doubting her value as a beloved daughter of the King of Kings. Still, Emma Mae refuses to retaliate. She chooses to believe what God says about her, which empowers her resilience as she extends loving forgiveness toward those who slash her with hurtful words. She keeps right on loving Jesus and people. And she waits on God to fight on her behalf.

Faithfully spreading the gospel of Christ and encouraging others to embrace their differences and celebrate their uniqueness, Emma Mae shares God's truth with confidence in the Lord's promises. She shares her story in *ALL-CAPS YOU: A 30-Day Devotional toward Finding Joy in Who God Made You to Be*, and she waits expectantly for the Lord to keep on protecting her reputation. She continues to use Scripture to encourage others and build her own confidence. Emma Mae believes with all her might that God will always keep His word . . . and she believes in the supremacy of His timely words, too.

God spoke the world into existence, miracle after miracle planned and paced by the maker and sustainer of all (Genesis 1–2). The disciples witnessed the power of Jesus's words when He spoke life into Lazarus four days after his death (John 11). The centurion demonstrated his belief in the authority of the Lord's words when he sent "elders" and then "friends" to meet Jesus in Capernaum and plead for healing on behalf of his servant (Luke 7:1–10). These biblical testimonies refresh Emma Mae's persevering heart and help develop her resilience. She rests in God's promises and relies on God's wisdom. She takes God at

His word. Standing on the reliability of His truth, she remembers that her identity, her value, and her enduring hope are in Christ . . . especially when the journey seems too hard and the wait feels endless.

I wish I could say I always handle attacks on my character as well as Emma does. A while ago, a woman confessed to gossiping about me after she ended our friendship. Knowing I'm still learning how to be a godly friend, I opened my heart to hear a hard truth. "Better is open rebuke than hidden love" (Proverbs 27:5). I braced myself, but she refused to tell me what I'd done to upset her in the first place.

Shocked by the loss of someone I considered a friend, I struggled with the grieving process. For months, I prayed, I cried, and I doubted my value as a friend . . . as a person. As time passed and God continued to answer me with silence, my sorrow simmered into a not-so-righteous anger. It wasn't fair. I deserved to know what I'd done to warrant this treatment. I wanted to compile a list of everyone who listened to her gossip disguised as venting and prayer requests. I longed to set the record straight.

I prayed, pleading for the truth to come to light, begging for justice and vindication. But instead of giving me permission to stone my ex-friend with jagged rocks of humiliation, God whispered, "Wait." The more I prayed, the more He brought verses to mind that nudged me to extend grace. As the Lord continued to work beyond my realm of understanding, He softened my heart to forgive . . . with or without an apology from my offender.

A few months later, another woman accused me of something I didn't do. When another relationship ended, my heart ached. Just when God was opening doors for more incredible ministry opportunities, I was losing the friends I depended on for support. Right before I spiraled into a why-me whine-fest, my faithful Lord and Savior assured me that my worth was revealed in His Word, not in what others said about me. God's purpose would prevail in the wait. He would keep His word. He would protect my heart and my reputation. He would provide the support I needed as I continued to focus on loving Him as He empowered me to love others . . . even when I didn't feel loved in return.

Since then, God has surrounded me with wonderful praying friends and colleagues, folks I'd known for years. Losing those two friends hurt, but the loss allowed me the time to nurture other relationships and venture down paths I wouldn't have had the courage to consider before.

Most of us have been stung by negative voices, hurtful words, gossip, and even false accusations. When we're tempted to doubt our value, to question God's leading, or to prove our rightness, we can look to the Lord for comfort and trust what He says about us. God chooses His words carefully, so we can stand on His Word confidently. During the ongoing waiting seasons of life, we have unlimited access to the moment-by-moment testimonies of faithfulness recorded in the infallible God-breathed words of Scripture. No matter how long or how hard our journey feels, we can worship the Lord with surety. We can count on Him to fight on our behalf. We can proclaim the authority of His Word with centurion-strong faith . . . just like young Emma Mae.

INHALE

For the LORD gives wisdom;
from his mouth come
knowledge and understanding.
—PROVERBS 2:6

EXHALE

Faithful Redeemer, please make us more like you. Give us a desire to feed our hearts and minds with your truth daily so we can discern your truth amidst the lies that try to deceive us.

When negative voices attack our character, please bring our minds back to the guarantee of your goodness and intentional creativity in creating us. Give us reassurance that your opinion of us is established by your unconditional love for us and your intimate knowledge of us, Lord.

Please strengthen our faith with every testimony that confirms your reliability as you care for us and fight on our behalf. Help us speak with love and grace when we respond to others, especially when we're feeling hurt or attacked.

Please, Lord, equip us to move forward, to let go, and to trust when you're working in ways we can't understand. Help us take you at your word and find comfort in your absolute trustworthiness.

In Jesus's name, Amen.

- Why is it hard to wait for God to handle our reputations when we're feeling attacked?

- What lies or opinions of others have you chosen to believe about yourself?

- How can knowing what God says about us help increase our confidence and courage as we wait for Him to work in and through our situations?

Truth-telling Father,
help us believe what you say.

5

Resting in God's Refuge

TODAY'S TRUTH

We can lose the things of this world,
but we can never lose God's love and presence.

TODAY'S READING: *Psalm 34:1–22*

Terminated. After almost a decade of award-winning service, Alan received an email from his employer informing him that his position had been eliminated due to a corporate restructure. The sole provider for our family, my hard-working husband was losing his job and, with it, our much-needed medical insurance.

About three months later, my back injury flared up. I thanked God Alan was home as I lay facedown on the floor writhing in pain. A visit to an orthopedic surgeon led to a long-awaited diagnosis. I would require multiple surgeries and procedures in my upper back, shoulders, and neck.

How were we going to pay for my treatments?

Without hesitation or complaint, Alan used our savings to pay for my unforeseen medical expenses and daily medication that amounted to hundreds of dollars per month.

His stellar education and experience would land him a job in no time. What could possibly go wrong?

I prayed with great expectations as Alan filled out application after application and waited. Silence. Overqualified. Silence. Fifty percent pay cut. Gulp. Wading through a flood of rejections, we paid each month's bills from our dwindling savings account. Month after month, we praised God for His ongoing provision. We waited for the miracle we anticipated right around the corner.

I clenched my jaw as I watched Alan writing check after check. "Are you sure you want to pay tithe this month?"

My husband kept a solid stride of faith when my knees trembled. He quoted his favorite verse with a calm courage I still admire. "Wait patiently for the LORD. Be brave and courageous. Yes, wait patiently for the LORD" (Psalm 27:14 NLT).

I hid behind a flimsy smile and flimsier faith, as he doled out funds for tithing, rent, bills, and medical expenses. The emotional turmoil and chronic pain wore me down. Fear trickled in when I lay awake in my recliner at night. I pleaded for relief.

Desperate for security, I turned to Jesus. Over the years, He'd proven He would never change and never fail. God would never let me down . . . even when I feared and even when my attempts to fix our situation failed miserably.

After ten months of unemployment, on a Friday afternoon, Alan announced we would have less than one hundred dollars in our account after paying our current monthly expenses. He clung to God's trustworthiness and remained resilient. I, on the other hand, winced as he wrote checks for the week's bills and tithe.

Oh, Lord, how are we were going to make our last seventy dollars stretch?

We? As the Holy Spirit gently reminded me of Scriptures that proved I could count on my heavenly Father, I confessed my nail-biting faith. Settling into the wait . . . with a bit of squirming when my nerves got the best of me . . . I worshipped God. *Help me believe you'll work even when I feel like we're at a standstill, Lord.*

After church that following Sunday, people who had never met each other shared how the Lord had placed our family on their hearts. I received their financial offerings with tears of thankfulness. Those gifts covered all . . . all . . . all of our March bills, including gas and groceries.

On Monday, a family friend called to ask if Alan was interested in a job. The recruiter contacted him, set up an interview at the airport, and hired him before the end of the week. Though he took a huge pay cut, we would have benefits and enough to cover our monthly bills. I shouted from the social-media mountaintop, declaring God's never-ending goodness, faithfulness, and perfect timing. *Oh, what a glorious God we serve! I never doubted Him . . . well, maybe I did for a minute or two.*

Before we could take a breath, though, my health took a nosedive. I could have raced back into the worry-zone, but something *in me* had changed.

Sifting through the book of Psalms, I slowed to read David's response to one of his seemingly big fails. While running from Saul's attacks, David succumbed to fear and feigned insanity when facing Achish, king of Gath (described in 1 Samuel 21:10–15). But even at one of his lowest points, David praised God.

"I will extol the LORD at all times; his praise will always be on my lips. I will glory in the LORD; let the afflicted hear and rejoice" (Psalm 34:1–2). David sang his testimony of reliance on the Lord Almighty. He invited others to give glory to our Helper and rejoice over His promised deliverance.

David's song rings with declarations of God as our refuge and provider. Whether struggling with sin, brokenhearted, or crushed in spirit, David remained confident that God could and would rise in all His magnificence to rescue those who honor Him. The psalmist sang with calm resolution, "The righteous person may have many troubles, but the LORD delivers him from them *all*" (v. 19, emphasis mine).

All. God is reliable. All. He can handle every last one of our pesky problems, no matter how big or how small. He can meet our deepest needs, quenching our thirst and replenishing our faith even when our well has run dry. According to His trust-worthy character, God transforms our prayers from desperate pleas for provision to grateful praises for His *promised* provision. We can expect Him to take care of us because His Word says that He will. He is *Jehovah-Jireh*, a name that means God Will Provide. Waiting won't always be easy or worry-free, but the process can lead to joyful expectation of God's dependability and the glorious exaltation of His name.

When the wait overwhelms us, it's perfectly natural for our first response to be a desperate cry for a break. Most wise folks want to escape tough times and avoid long treks through dry valleys. We desire instant gratification, even when we recognize the value in the wait. We don't have to deny those weaknesses exist. Like David, we can be real with God. As we process our emotions with Spirit-empowered resilience, we can praise Him. We can expect Him to stay true to His infallible Word and His unchanging character as the clock tick-tocks away. Each moment in the wait brings us closer to the day we stand before His throne, forever worshipping Him and sheltered by His eternal presence.

INHALE

> Taste and see that the LORD is good;
> blessed is the one who takes refuge in him.
> —PSALM 34:8

EXHALE

Lord, we praise you. We trust you for refuge, for deliverance. We know you hear us. Thanks for providing all we need in accordance with your perfect plan and flawless timing. Please shelter us with your faithfulness. Relieve our minds of this world's worries as we trust in your all-knowing goodness, compassion, and love.

Help us feel your constant and powerful presence as you keep us safe in the center of your will. When fear, anxiety, and the impossibilities of our circumstances create doubt, please draw us to your Word and help us lean into your promises.

You are our Lord, our King, our maker and sustainer. You are our protector and provider. Without you, we have no good thing, Lord. But with you, even though we have no idea where or how or when, we can trust you are going to meet our deepest needs. Please help us trust you.

In Jesus's name, Amen.

- How has God helped you or a friend through a time of financial, physical, or emotional need?

- How can sharing your testimony or hearing the testimonies of others increase the faith of those who are struggling with a lack of worldly security as they wait on God to provide?

- In what situation can you trust the Lord's promised provision and protection this week?

Merciful Father,
you are a refuge
more soul-satisfying
than any pleasure
or relief on this earth.

6

Enough for the Wait

TODAY'S TRUTH

Knowing God intimately helps us trust
He's more than enough today and forever.

TODAY'S READING: *2 Corinthians 12:1–10*

I noticed Patricia's genuine smile before I even glanced at her sparkly gown. She stepped slowly across the banquet room, sequins glinting as she moved, and hugged the newly wedded couple. Glancing my way, she waved me over to a table in the far corner of the room. I rose from my chair and walked toward her, mesmerized by the peacefulness of her face. I could feel my cheeks stretching into a huge grin as joy bubbled up in my heart.

As I arrived at her table, Patricia lifted her shaky twig-arms and took off her fancy hat. Wisps of hair clung to her balding head. "Wigs itch," she said with a glint in her eyes. "And hats make my head sweaty, so please forgive my appearance."

With a smile spread across her face, all I saw was loveliness. Patricia had been trusting the Lord through a fierce battle against cancer. Her phenomenal faith gave her a glow. She knew she didn't have much time left on this side of eternity, so she took every opportunity to share how Jesus was working in and through her life.

I listened as she shared her most recent trust tally—the list of every time God had provided for her, protected her, and blessed her with peace when pain overwhelmed her. I should have taken notes. She took breaks as she spoke, smiling often and using "Praise the Lord" as a period, a comma, and an exclamation point.

Feeling foolish for complaining about my bouts with chronic pain earlier that day, I said, "You inspire me, Ms. Patricia."

"That's Jesus, sweetheart. It's all Jesus." My beautiful sister in Christ leaned toward me. "I see Him in you, too." She placed her trembling hand in mine and squeezed. "I'll be seeing Him face-to-face, soon, you know. I want you to come to my home and pray for me. But for now, let's enjoy the celebration."

Ms. Patricia didn't stay long after our exchange and I didn't wait long to make that home-visit. Still, she was bedridden by the time I walked through her front door. Her frail body lay still on the right side of the bed, tucked in with love by a daughter who beamed with the same great faith. "Mom's been waiting for you," she said. "She's ready to go Home."

I lay next to her, hugged her thin arm, and gently pressed my head against her frail shoulder. With a raspy voice, she breathed a blessing over me and my husband who kneeled at the edge of the bed. He held her hand and bowed his head as I began praying through tears. I thanked God for Ms. Patricia's beautiful life, through which He had demonstrated His goodness, faithfulness, and timely provision. Though He didn't relieve my friend's pain, He gave her enough for the wait. Enough grace. Enough strength. Enough courage. Enough hope. Whatever she required, God gave her enough. When she felt like she was still lacking and struggling to get by, His presence, His love, His promises were enough because she knew He was enough. In return, Patricia shared God with others, loving people as His love flowed generously in and through her life. She made a difference in so many lives and gave God all the glory He rightly deserved.

The apostle Paul, like Ms. Patricia, knew the Lord had done marvelous works, deeds so marvelous that he couldn't keep himself from boasting in His might and mercy (2 Corinthians 12:1–6). Paul proudly declared his own weaknesses, in hopes to magnify the power of God and prevent folks from thinking "too highly" of him . . . a mere servant of the Lord (v. 6). He accepted his suffering—his "thorn in the flesh" as many versions say— as an opportunity to highlight Christ's goodness and majesty. All the while, he acknowledged his own smallness in the grand scheme of things on this side of eternity.

Paul never claimed to enjoy suffering. On the contrary, he admitted to praying for relief multiple times. But then he accepted the Lord's response: "My kindness is all you need. My power is strongest when you are weak" (v. 9 CEV). In an incredible act of worship, the apostle declared, "So if Christ keeps giving me his power, I will gladly brag about how weak I am. Yes, I am glad to be weak or insulted or mistreated or to have troubles and sufferings, if it is for Christ. Because when I am weak, I am strong" (vv. 9–10 CEV).

Over the years, some have criticized me for having weak faith because my chronic pain persists and doctors continue to be flabbergasted by the extent of my injury and the lack of viable treatments. When I'm tempted to believe those critics, I consider all Ms. Patricia suffered physically, emotionally, and mentally. When she was weak, God remained her strength. She brought glory to His name when she shared how He carried her through each day. When I'm weak, God doesn't just give me strength . . . He *is* my strength. This rock-solid stone of truth bolsters the foundation of my faith.

I'm not waiting for the Lord to give me relief anymore. I'm not waiting for Him to stop the pain or lead me to a doctor that will solve the great mystery surrounding my injury and the treatment required. I haven't given up on these hopes. However, the main focus of my wait has shifted. I'm waiting *for* God. I'm waiting for Him to reveal himself to me as He works in and through my life. I'm waiting for Him to guide my steps. I'm waiting for Him to provide all I need in order to do all He sets before me. I'm waiting for Him to refine me through the journey. While I wait for God, I *will* experience suffering, have mini-meltdowns, and cry out for relief. I *will* want to give up and I *will* feel overwhelmed when the pain won't let up. But just as Paul and Ms. Patricia remained steadfast, I *will* wait in God's presence and fully expect He will give me enough. Enough grace. Enough strength. Enough peace. Enough courage. Whatever I require, God will give me enough. More importantly, He'll help me believe His ongoing presence is enough, His love is enough, His peace is enough, His hope is enough, simply because *He* is enough.

Each of us will walk through seemingly endless valleys of discouragement, weariness, heartache, or pain. Still, we can boast in the Lord's greatness and remember His faithfulness never fails us. We can experience joy and peace that do not depend on the measure of weariness or difficulties in our lives. Nothing can satisfy us more than our Rock, our holy and loving Lord. So when the wait feels unbearable, we don't have to walk with hunched shoulders or long faces, filled with bitterness and spouting complaints. We can rise up in victory or lie down in the peace of His presence. No matter how much the world insists we're defeated, we can persevere and know God is and always will be enough.

INHALE

My flesh and my heart may fail,
but God is the strength of my heart
and my portion forever.
—PSALM 73:26

EXHALE

Powerful Sustainer, thanks for knowing we are weak, for understanding we will grow weary, for caring when we worry that we won't have enough. Thanks for helping us walk with confidence as you lead us into the everlasting. Convict us when we are tempted to rely on our own strength, our own abilities, our own accomplishments.

Please help us fearlessly face what lies ahead, even when the wait drags on or stretches our boundary lines way past our comfort zones.

When we tire of waiting, please shift our focus from our current situation to your constant presence. Help us know with all of our hearts that you will provide for our needs as you help us acknowledge how much we need you above all else, Lord.

In Jesus's name, Amen.

- When is it hardest to remember that being in Jesus's presence is enough?

- Why is it often hard to admit we need God?

- Whose testimony has God used to help you place one more rock-solid stone of truth in the foundation of your faith?

Perfect Savior,
you are always enough.

7

F.R.O.G. Faith

TODAY'S TRUTH

*We can be fully reliant on God
when we know He's fully reliable.*

TODAY'S READING: *Hebrews 11*

After my flare-ups triggered increased muscle spasms, nerve pain, and headaches, I needed something big to motivate me to get up and move. My husband and I signed up for Walk to End Alzheimer's in honor of his mother, who suffered from this debilitating disease. We gathered donations and organized a team of walkers to join us. After meeting our team at the registration table, I had a difficult time hiding my pain. The muscles in my back spasmed and my headache increased in severity. Discouraged, I chose to walk the short trail while my team stuck together on the longer path.

I strolled with a group of slow-walking strangers. Praying for pain management so I could finish the challenge, I shared a smile and polite conversation with people as they passed me. As I rounded the first corner, I saw a curly-haired pup being pulled in a large red wagon decorated with crepe-paper flowers and butterflies. An older gentleman introduced himself and began telling me stories about his World War II adventures. Bob repeated the same story, each time grinning wider when I engaged with him. His wife, Beth, held a bouquet of handmade flowers as she quietly kept in step with her husband. Their daughter apologized, explaining that her dad suffered from Alzheimer's.

I waved off her apology. "I'm enjoying every minute of our conversation," I said.

After we crossed the short-path finish line, we settled into a shady spot on a nearby bench. Bob rearranged the fake flowers in the wagon and rubbed their sweet pup behind the ears. "These are five dollars each," he said, handing me a purple flower with a blue butterfly glued onto the top of the tissue-petals.

I bought two and grinned as Bob joined his daughter to sell the rest of the bouquet.

Beth sat beside me. She set a stuffed white envelope on her lap. "Do you know Jesus?"

My heart fluttered with joy. "Yes, ma'am."

Her face beamed as she opened the envelope and slipped out a crisp dollar bill. "Good. Then you'll know how the story ends." She shared the gospel with me as she folded the bill origami-style. "Fully Reliant on God," she said, glancing toward her husband. "That's the only way we're going to make it."

Tears slipped down my cheeks when she handed me the small paper frog she'd created. "Thanks," I said. "I needed that reminder." I spent the rest of the afternoon talking to Beth about how faithful God is and always will be. My pain didn't lessen. My headache didn't ease up. But my refreshed spirit enabled me to embrace the truth my sister in Christ had shared with me. God was bigger than my pain, bigger than Bob's diagnosis, bigger than Beth's grief as she loved her husband well. God's abilities surpass our greatest needs. He would remain reliable, even when we couldn't see an end to our hardships.

Just like the Old Testament God-followers in the Bible's so-called Hall of Faith (Hebrews 11), Beth's vigorous faith bloomed from the sureness in what she hoped for and the certainty about what she could not see—God's reliability—whether or not she saw an end to her suffering. Her trust in the Lord mirrored the depth of faith the ancients were "commended for" (vv. 1–2). As we begin to grasp the reality of God as creator of the universe, we can begin to believe in His bigness and dependability to run the world. The Lord can manage every detail of every situation . . . including the hardest moments we'll ever face. We can rely on Him through every second of the seemingly endless waiting seasons in life.

Living by faith, Noah faced ridicule; he trusted the Lord when it made no sense to critical bystanders. By faith, Abraham followed God into the unknown; he ventured toward the Lord's voice, willing to be a foreigner living in a tent surrounded by strangers. Abraham followed the Lord without demanding to know all the details, without expecting comfort. He didn't concern himself with how long or rocky the road ahead would be, "for he was looking forward to the city with foundations, whose architect and builder is God" (v. 10). Heaven, the ultimate Promised Land. Abraham believed God because he depended on God's immeasurable goodness, established faithfulness, limitless power, and relentless mercy. Abraham knew that his wife's physical limitations or diagnosis of infertility didn't determine God's reliability.

The Hall of Faith includes portraits of those who trusted the Lord until they died. In a glorious picture of faith in action, God affirms the need for our reliance on Him and our interdependence within the community of believers past and present. Their diligent and courageous faith in His trustworthiness throughout every moment of the wait inspires our persistence. Their stories meld with ours in a beautiful collage of testimonies. The same God who works in and through each second of our waiting seasons is the same God who saved Moses as a baby and determined each twist and turn in his complicated life as a kid adopted by the Pharaoh's daughter.

The list of faith-warriors could go on and on. Their wait wasn't always comfortable or even semi-pleasurable. "Some faced jeers and flogging, and even chains and imprisonment" (v. 36). Some became wanderers and "none of them received what had been promised" (vv. 37–39). None. Not one. Still, they waited with steadfast faith, "since God had planned something better for us so that only together with us would they be made perfect" (v. 40). As we seek the Lord and follow His leading on this side of eternity, we can count on His consistency. We can learn to receive the fullness of His unconditional love for us. We can serve Him and tell others about Him. And we can rest in His loving kindness . . . until we join Him in His eternal glory. We can review the ongoing testimonies of our brothers and sisters in Christ and create an endless list of His proven faithfulness, goodness, and dependability. We can be fully reliant on God. His unchanging character and unconditional love for us remain secured in who He is and always will be, not in our ability to believe or even our capacity to remember He is a keeper of His Word.

God paves the path ahead of us. He goes before us, remaining with us and protecting us on all sides. With confidence abounding, we can expect Him to wrap us in limitless love and more-than-sufficient grace. As the Lord gives us hope to rely on Him completely and confidently in and through all circumstances, patience becomes an act of worship, not a measure of our faith. We can rejoice in being grounded in the certainty that the Maker of all things, including time, has a perfect plan and pace. The Lord has established and fully intends to use every moment of the wait to refine us into His likeness, to bring glory to His name, and to magnify the persevering power of His promises.

INHALE

> Now faith is confidence in what we hope for
> and assurance about what we do not see.
>
> —HEBREWS 11:1

EXHALE

Creator and Sustainer, we love you and are grateful for your proven trustworthiness. Your faithfulness never falters. Your consistency never fails. Your goodness never depends on our ability to believe.

We can't walk in confident faith without you, Lord. Please remind us that you won't forget us, even when we forget you. Please help us remember the ways you've shown yourself to be reliable, the countless examples of your promise-keeping.

When our struggles don't seem to have an end in sight, please empower us to rise up in grace-filled peace. Help us stroll through the pathways you've prepared for us with steadfast hope.

Please increase our trust through the testimonies of those who are fully reliant on you, God. Mold us into the mighty faith-warriors you intend us to be, the proclaimers of your truth and the lovers of your people you've commanded us to be.

Empower us to take F.R.O.G.-leaps of faith as we face each moment of the wait with our eyes fixed on you and your promises.

In Jesus's name, Amen.

- How can considering God as creator and sustainer of all help us trust He won't forget us, even when we forget Him in the wait?

- What situation are you dealing with that seems to have no end in sight?

- What makes it most difficult to be fully reliant on God when your circumstances don't seem to be improving on this side of eternity?

Holy Spirit, thanks for empowering us to trust you.

8
Deliberate Delays and Detours

TODAY'S TRUTH

God's planning includes timely, deliberate,
faith-strengthening delays and detours.

TODAY'S READING: *Mark 9:14–29*

After weeks filled with appointments while serving as my
mom's live-in caregiver at the cancer care center, I grew weary
of watching her suffering. I'd asked the doctors to help relieve
her pain . . . but they could not. Desperate for refreshment, I sat
down to read the Bible and pray. But I struggled to stay awake.
Hopelessness and loneliness seeped into my heart as I dealt with
the mixed emotions of feeling far from God and being separated
from family, friends, and my church. Still, I had to be strong for
my mom.

I had to maintain the high level of cheerfulness she needed
to encourage her when weariness overcame her. I couldn't let
her see me bent under the weight of my emotional weakness or
overwhelmed by my own chronic pain. I couldn't let her see me
in the middle of a poor-me meltdown or pushed over the edge
by frustration over setbacks I couldn't control. How could she
trust me to care for her if I couldn't even take care of myself?

At the end of a rough week, I blinked back tears and did my
best to make my mom comfortable. I needed an excuse to leave
the room. "I'll be right back," I said.

My mom strained to roll over on the bed. "Where are you going?"

I reassured my tired mama with a smile. Trying to keep my voice from quavering, I said, "I forgot to take out the meat for dinner." It wasn't a lie, or my main reason for leaving. The community kitchen had a pantry I had used as a prayer closet . . . and a sobbing shelter. Before my mom could insist on joining me, I zipped out of our room, down the hallway, and into the elevator. As soon as the doors closed, I started crying. *How much longer, Lord? I know you can help us.*

Did I really, though? The thought triggered a whirlpool of guilt and grief. When had I stopped believing God would keep His Word? When had I stopped trusting His grace was enough to carry me through the long days I knew I'd be facing when I accepted the role as my mom's live-in caregiver? I entered the community kitchen and inwardly groaned when I heard laughter. I planned to pretend to be preoccupied, so I could avoid the cheerful cooks and also resist the temptation of locking myself in the pantry and having a total meltdown.

As I walked through the room faster than necessary, one of the women spoke. "Hey, do you know where they keep the strainer?"

Taking a deep breath, I pasted on a friendly smile and turned toward her. My eyes grazed over her bandages, the telltale sign of a patient. *What's wrong with me, Lord? Please forgive me. Help me encourage her.* "Nothing is ever in the same place twice," I said.

Within minutes, we were sharing our stories and praising the Lord together. As Keilah waited on God for a heart transplant, an unexpected schedule change led the hospital to provide a one-night stay at the cancer care house. God determines the details and purposes of all life's delays and detours. That day, our dependable Father brought Keilah, her sister, and her brother-in-law to that community kitchen to minister to my weary spirit. He knew I needed my hope revitalized. He knew I needed a reminder of His all-knowing goodness. I needed assurance of His limitless reach, His mind-boggling bigness, and His soul-refreshing mercy.

After proclaiming God's awesome wonders and testifying how His love changed each of our lives, we held hands and brought our concerns before the Lord together . . . in the community kitchen of the cancer house. Only God! Only God could arrange such a wonderful delay that led to the meeting that still deepens my faith today.

I didn't want to admit self-sufficiency had triggered my weariness and uncertainty. I had stopped resting in God's presence, refreshing my spirit with His Word, and relying on His power. When the wait seemed endless, I had stopped trusting God's faithfulness and being confident in what I so-easily preached to others.

Sure, I'd prayed. But my pleas were like those of the desperate father in Mark 9. After years of watching his son suffer, he'd tried to be Mr. Fixer and failed. He'd gone to the disciples for help. They failed. Scripture doesn't tell us how much time passed before that dad pushed his way through a crowd and cried out to Jesus. But time passed. The strain of his wait continued. Once he stood face-to-face with the Lord, he explained his son's ongoing pain. I can only imagine the ache in his voice as he tried to contain his grief. "I asked your disciples to drive out the spirit, but they could not" (v. 18).

Without hesitation, Jesus nudged the father into a deliberate detour. "Bring the boy to me," He said (v. 19).

Why did the father ask the disciples for help before coming straight to Jesus?

Why did I let so much time pass before I brought my broken heart and empty spirit to Jesus?

Why didn't I admit my desperation, grab my mom's hands that night, and bring her to Jesus through intercessory prayer?

I still can't answer those questions. But as I think back on that encounter with God and my new community-kitchen friends, I can appreciate the necessity and value of the delays and detours He uses to deepen our faith.

Jesus—sovereign and strong—invited that hurting father in Mark 9 to vent, to confirm the impossibility of his son's situation. The father admitted he'd watched his son suffer "from childhood" (v. 21). Scripture doesn't tell us his son's age, but the father's simple answer confirmed years, possibly decades of heartache. How many times did he hide from his family, silencing heart-wrenching sobs, wishing his son could speak? How many times did he watch in horror, feeling helpless as his son fell into fierce seizure-like attacks? How many times did he try to be strong for his son, hiding his weakness and sucking up his own pain? How long did it take for his discouragement to dwindle into doubt?

The father stood before Jesus and said, "But *if* you can do anything, take pity on us and help us" (v. 22, emphasis mine).

"'If you can?'" said Jesus. "Everything is possible for one who believes" (v. 23).

After he had lived for years in fear-filled faith, a glimmer of hope ignited this man's desire to trust the Lord. "Immediately the boy's father exclaimed, 'I do believe; help me overcome my unbelief'" (v. 24).

Jesus healed his son right before his eyes. The Lord himself freed this desperate parent from the chains of unbelief and armed him with a shield of faith. Admitting his inability to endure the wait without God's help, this father became an intercessory prayer warrior. As he watched his son suffer with no relief in sight, how could he have even imagined such a glorious day?

In our DIY world, children of God don't have to be do-it-ourselves disciples. The Holy Spirit gives us the power to be dependent on Him during every delay and detour He weaves into our lives.

INHALE

Let us run with endurance the race
that is set before us, looking to Jesus,
the founder and perfecter of our faith.

—HEBREWS 12:1–2 ESV

EXHALE

*Faithful Restorer and Deliverer, thanks for reminding us that we can
do nothing—not even believe you—without your help. Please reveal
when we're trying to be do-it-yourself disciples and forgive us for falling
into the temptation of self-sufficiency.*

*Please help us surrender to you as an act of faith in your unchanging
character and your ability to do all things.*

*Help us come to you daily, so you can refill our souls with your
heart-transforming Word before we're physically, emotionally, mentally,
and spiritually drained.*

*Give us the courage to kneel before you and bring our hurting loved
ones before you with certainty in your limitless power.*

*We believe, Lord. But we confess that our faith is often weak. We
know you are the one who establishes the foundation on which our faith
is built. Only you can help us with our unbelief. So help us, Lord.
Enable us to live like we believe everything you say. Give us all we
need to live like we know your promises will come to fruition as we
trust daily in your perfect plan and pace.*

In Jesus's name, Amen.

- In what situation are you trying to be a do-it-yourself disciple?

- Why does it seem harder to surrender and rely on God when we see no end to our suffering?

- In what area of your life do you need to cry out to the Lord and say, "I believe; help me with my unbelief"?

Great God, we come to you
because we can depend on you.

9

The Pace for Preparation

TODAY'S TRUTH
The Lord never rushes
our refining process.

TODAY'S READING: *1 Samuel 16*

My husband and I enjoy mentoring teens and have had the pleasure and privilege of serving as youth ministry leaders for over a
decade. In an effort to help our students nurture a love for God's
Word by developing a habit of reading Scripture, we started a
Bible Challenge program. We invited the teens to prayerfully
dig into the Bible. We quizzed them to make sure they did the
assigned readings and rewarded them with a party at the end of
the challenge.

When we added Galatians to our schedule, I used construc-
tion paper to create a Fruit of the Spirit Tree on the youth room
wall. We invited church members, parents, teachers, and community members to inform us when they witnessed our students
living out the fruits of the Spirit: "love, joy, peace, forbearance,
kindness, goodness, faithfulness, gentleness and self-control"
(Galatians 5:22–23). As the weeks rolled by, the emails and calls
rolled in with stories of how each student walked with the Spirit
as they studied the book of Galatians.

I wrote the students' names and a short description of their
actions on fruit die-cuts. Eventually, those flat-fruit testimonies

of our students' faithfulness in Christ filled our tree. I praised the Lord as I overheard several teens raving about how much they enjoyed loving God by loving people. I thanked the Lord for working in their hearts when I witnessed some of our shy students stepping up and using their God-given gifts to serve at church and in our community. They could have refused to participate, but by God's incredible grace, those awesome teens honored the Lord through every week of our Galatians Bible Challenge. They chose to serve others "humbly in love" (Galatians 5:13–14).

Thrilled about how our students were putting feet to their faith, I was shocked when one of the parents told me the Bible Challenge program was useless. "They're only doing these things to earn a party," he said. "There is no real spiritual growth happening."

I assured him God would cultivate their growth in His timing. According to His perfect plan, and regardless of our motivations at any particular time, training in God's Word always has the potential to bear fruit.

Since then, I've watched those students grow into amazing adults. I don't know if our Bible Challenge had anything to do with their spiritual growth. I don't know if any of the time I invested in them made a difference in their walk with the Lord. But I do know the Lord used that experience to help *me* grow and to help *me* see the value of intentionally studying and applying His Word.

I learned that spiritual growth is a lifetime process and that God's timing is purposeful and necessary as He prepares us for all He has in store for us. God, the Maker of time, is not a time-waster. He knows when we're ready to step into the next phase of the plan He's designed for us and when we need more time to prepare. He also knows how easily we forget our lives are entwined with the lives of others—those we know, strangers, and those yet to come. The Lord orchestrates every twist and turn and pit stop in our lives, as well as the paths He has set for every other person He loves. God's plans take time to unfold. I can imagine no one knows that better than David.

The Lord directed the prophet Samuel to anoint the teenage David as the future king of Judah (1 Samuel 16:12–13). Though David seemed to be an unlikely leader, even a poor choice, Scripture reminds us God isn't shortsighted. He sees beyond the surface, past our facades, and into the potential He's placed in each and every one of us. "The LORD does not look at the things people look at. People look at the outward appearance, but the LORD looks at the heart" (1 Samuel 16:7). Only God knew that David was chosen but definitely not ready to fulfill his life's purpose, yet.

After David received his anointing, God began His good work in the one who would eventually be called "a man after God's own heart" (see 1 Samuel 13:14; Acts 13:22). David needed to develop his leadership skills and have his character refined a bit. As he tended his father's sheep, he honed skills that he'd eventually need to face a giant. As he stepped up to Goliath during a battle with the Philistines, he had opportunity to practice both humility and courage, traits he'd need to fend off his persecutor, Saul. As he experienced rejection from this jealous king (while still trying to respect Saul's God-given authority), he stood up to those who tried to persuade him to murder Saul. He exercised his inner strength against opposition when his commitment to obeying God wasn't popular with those around him. God used these experiences and more to help develop David's character and diminish his self-reliance before David could step into his role as king. And of course, his spiritual growth didn't stop there.

Spiritual refinement requires a lifetime of surrender to God's supreme power and all-encompassing knowledge, a willingness to wait for Him to set each piece of His plan in place. God knows the perfect pace required to maximize our potential. We may get antsy when the process takes longer than we expected or is harder than we'd imagined. Still, we can trust God always has good reasons when planning every detail in every priceless life He has created. Love never wastes time or rushes us toward the next step one second before we're fully prepared to follow Him and finish well.

INHALE

The plans of the LORD stand firm forever,
the purposes of his heart
through all generations.
—PSALM 33:11

EXHALE

All-Knowing and All-Loving Father, thanks for knowing what's best for us.

Thanks for taking your time to develop the potential you've placed in us and never rushing us or giving in to our demands when we're impatient.

Please help us trust your judgment, your guidance, and your perfect timing.

Please, Father, help us embrace the process you've planned for our spiritual growth and trust you to decide how that process connects to those around us. Keep us from focusing on our failures or dwelling on how much more we need to grow. Instead, help us approach each day as an opportunity to draw closer to you, to fall deeper in love with you. Help us live for you and honor you as you make us more like Jesus Christ.

Please continue to build our character so that we reflect the Son. Lord, please equip us for the path and pace you have determined is just right for us.

In Jesus's name, Amen.

- How do you feel when someone says you're not ready to do something God has placed on your heart to do?

- Describe a time when you jumped ahead of God and took on a role you weren't ready for or a role that wasn't meant for you.

- How does knowing that God includes preparation time in His planning help you trust Him when the wait feels endless?

Sovereign Lord,
please help us trust your timing.

10

Able and Available

TODAY'S TRUTH

*God helps us focus on His ability and availability
to be our strength and peace.*

TODAY'S READING: *Daniel 3*

When Lyla came into this world with her umbilical cord wrapped around her neck, doctors pronounced her dead three times. Though she survived, she suffered from a lack of oxygen that caused cerebral palsy. As a little girl, Lyla loved Jesus, but it wasn't until her junior year in high school that God fanned the flames of her faith. When a preacher visited her youth group and prayed with her, Lyla dedicated her life to Christ and soon headed to a Christian college.

Reflecting on the years she endured increasing physical limitations, she remembers taking a Human Development class and learning about the natural growth of babies. "I was sad because I missed being able to do what they did," she said. "Then I got mad at the doctor, which is all part of grief." Pausing for a moment, she took a breath. "I had to forgive him."

I considered my own healing journey. I'd never forgiven the physical therapist who I believe caused my initial injury to worsen by forcing my rib back into place instead of ordering more tests. Convicted, I asked Lyla how she managed to forgive the doctor.

"Over the years, forgiveness has been getting easier, but it's not *easy*. That's okay with God, though. Every time we struggle, He changes our hearts. He wants us to be truthful with Him."

If my aching body would have cooperated, I would've jumped up and shouted, "Hallelujah!" When I first accepted Christ as my Savior, I had no idea it was okay for me to be honest about my struggles, to admit the wait was hard, to confess I couldn't walk by faith on my own. Like Lyla, I had to find peace while waiting for God when living with a situation that may never get better. Though we both believe the Lord is able and available, we also know He won't always rescue us from life's fires. But no matter how hot or how long the flames of affliction burn, the Lord will walk with us and comfort us when we place our trust in Him.

"It's hard when there's a gap," Lyla said, "when we have to wait for God until He shows us the way."

Feeling the noose of conviction, I remembered the last visit with my doctor. Pain management might be the best he could offer me. Surgery may not be an option. Anger. Grief. Frustration. Discouragement. A surge of mixed emotions overwhelmed me and I swallowed hard. "What helps you in the gap, Lyla?"

"Surrender," she said. "I wrestle with God and then remember that He is doing other things in me and through me. That's why I wrote my book."

A friend had helped Lyla self-publish *It Takes More Than Legs to Stand*, in which she shares her story and testifies how God has helped her.

"A lot of people have shared how my story has helped them believe God more and trust God more," she said.

This sister in Christ had no idea the Lord was using her at that very moment. She inspired me to remain steadfast as I processed the latest diagnosis from my doctor. Her story encouraged me as I entered a new waiting season—my sojourn in the land of grief.

Lyla's mind-set does not permit her to just *survive* in her circumstances. Her disability didn't stop her from getting married, raising children, or loving on grandchildren. She has even been parasailing. Though she may struggle with daily tasks, she isn't defeated by anxiety or circumstance-driven fear. Instead, she struts around in her wheelchair with furnace-fire faith. No matter how intense the flames of adversity rage around her, Lyla believes God's promises. She knows He is able to do "immeasurably more" than anything she could ever imagine (Ephesians 3:20).

Furnace-fire faith provides a powerful witness to others. When King Nebuchadnezzar demanded all the people in Babylon bow down to a golden idol made in his image, Daniel 3 tells us that Shadrach, Meshach, and Abednego refused. The enraged king threatened God's faithful-three, but they stood firm. "King Nebuchadnezzar," they said, "we do not need to defend ourselves before you in this matter. If we are thrown into the blazing furnace, the God we serve *is able* to deliver us from it, and *he will* deliver us from Your Majesty's hand. *But even if he does not*, we want you to know, Your Majesty, that we will not serve your gods or worship the image of gold you have set up" (vv. 16–18, emphasis mine). These faithful Jews trusted the Lord to remain trustworthy through the wait . . . no matter how long, how hard, or how costly their journey would become.

The king ordered that Shadrach, Meshach, and Abednego be bound and thrown into a furnace that blazed so hot that the soldiers who carried out the sentence died at the door. Soon after, the king "leaped to his feet in amazement." He had noticed someone walking through the fire with them. Scripture doesn't tell us how long Shadrach, Meshach, and Abednego strolled around in those flames, but as they felt the heat . . . God was with them.

While it's tempting to just focus on what God did during their time in the fire, it's important to notice what God did *not* do: The Lord didn't snuff out the flames or make the furnace doors burst open. He didn't avenge their mistreatment or immediately strike the self-absorbed Babylonian king dead. God had the power to do these things, which makes it even more astounding when we notice what He chose to do: He kept the three calm and He preserved their lives. He assured them of His ongoing presence and walked with them during the wait. And the result? King Nebuchadnezzar realized God's greatness.

When the king called the three men out of the fire, those who witnessed the miracle gathered around them. "They saw that the fire had not harmed their bodies, nor was a hair of their heads singed; their robes were not scorched, and there was no smell of fire on them" (vv. 27). Seeing how God cared for Shadrach, Meshach, and Abednego in the blaze, witnessing His presence with them as they waited for God to move, King Nebuchadnezzar was led to praise the Lord. Their bold walk of faith changed them and those who observed them. And God still uses their testimony, as recorded and preserved in Scripture, to change and encourage us as we witness how God worked when the situation seemed hopeless.

As Lyla rests in the peace of the Lord's presence, He walks with her. When I feel the heat of my circumstances, God walks with me. No matter how many scars we hide, how many hopes we see dashed, how many fires threaten to consume us . . . God walks with us. God's ability isn't determined by our stability in the wait. Whether we're standing firm or stumbling along with our knees shaking, our mighty Lord is always available and always able. We may not be able to avoid the heat or escape the flames of adversity, but we can count on the Lord—the Promise Keeper—to walk with us in and through the blazes of life.

INHALE

My comfort in my suffering is this:
Your promise preserves my life.
—PSALM 119:50

EXHALE

Mighty King of Kings, thanks for helping us declare you as God above all. You understand that our moments of weakness, impatience, fear, and doubt are caused by our fleshly weakness.

Thanks for fueling us with peace that allows our faith to withstand the fiercest flames of adversity.

When the fires burn hot around us, protect us with the promise of your unconditional love and mercy. Shield us with your truth to combat the lies that tempt us toward idolatry. Encourage us with heat-enduring hope.

We can do nothing apart from you, merciful Promise Keeper. You alone preserve our lives. You sustain us by remaining close to us in all circumstances. Please help us walk with contagious joy and confidence that testifies of your proven faithfulness.

In Jesus's name, Amen.

- How can the assurance of God's presence fuel perseverance when you're walking through the fires of adversity?

- Why is it harder to trust the Lord when our situations don't change?

- How has God used someone else's bold faith to encourage you in your walk with Him?

All-powerful God,
thanks for being with us
and preserving us.

11

Wait Like a Warrior

TODAY'S TRUTH

*Waiting is an active verb that leads to a life
of enduring victory in Christ.*

TODAY'S READING: *Psalm 29*

I unwrapped the international package, intrigued that someone from the United Kingdom would take the time to send me
a gift. While the book was a treat, the handwritten card was
the treasure that God used to replenish my weary spirit. In the
note, Lynda apologized for her handwriting. She'd had multiple
strokes and had been relearning how to speak and write. Each
shaky line in her note reflected God's incredible faithfulness and
love for His beloved daughter.

Lynda and I occasionally email one another. I'm grateful for
her cheerful attitude and never-complaining spirit. Her grate-
fulness and compassion toward others fill me with hope and the
desire to encourage others with such selflessness. Her uplifting messages are rays of sunshine. Every word she writes with
unsteady hands is a testimony of her steadfast faith. She inspires
me to trust God when the wait is *guaranteed* to be endless, at least
on this side of eternity.

With limited mobility and a diagnosis that doesn't leave room
for the hope of regaining lost strength, apart from a miracle,
Lynda chooses to serve God and others with squiggly lines and

a shaky voice overflowing with conviction. She waits like a warrior, armed with grace-filled prayers for those who don't know the Lord, those who are suffering, and those she barely knows . . . like me.

When I get tired of going through each day with constant pain, I think of Lynda sitting in her wheelchair. She's hurting, continually, but happy to be allowed every opportunity to praise the Lord. She's selfless and generous, considering others more important than herself. She prays faithfully for people, knowing the reach of her intercessions is not limited by her physical limitations. Lynda shares how the Lord is holding her through the toughest days of her healing journey. Yes, she's on a healing journey.

She may not be expecting relief on this side of eternity, but Lynda is certainly waiting actively and expectantly for God's ultimate healing as He carries her through each day. She's not conceding to a half-life because of her physical limitations or her doctor's diagnosis. Rather, she continues to thrive in the life the Lord has given her. Multiple strokes have not taken away her heart for God or people. Pain has not diminished her hope or silenced her praise. Lynda trusts the God-breathed words of Scripture and rests in the surety of our High Priest's understanding. When there's no answer to the questions *why* or *how*, Lynda still praises God for His glory and strength. Then, she lifts up her shield of persevering faith.

Another waiting warrior, David, accepted the winding valley-trails God placed before him and marched onward with a spirit of worship. He wrote, "Ascribe to the LORD the glory due his name; worship the LORD in the splendor of his holiness" (Psalm 29:2). Even when his life was in danger, even when his bad choices caused his tough circumstances, David never failed to praise the Lord for who He was and always will be. He gave the Lord the glory due His name, which was basically a celebration of His attributes.

When we are hurting, we can meditate on these powerful names and give God the glory He is due:

- *El Shaddai*, the Lord God Almighty. (Psalm 91:1)
- *Adonai*, our Lord and Master. (Psalm 40:17; 71:5–6; 86:3)
- *Jehovah-Raah*, the Lord My Shepherd. (Psalm 23:1)
- *El Elyon*, the Most High God. (Psalm 57:2; 91:9)
- *El Olam*, Everlasting God. (Isaiah 26:4)

This is the Lord that David declared holy and worthy of all our worship.

- The Lord God Almighty reigns, omnipotent and supreme with unlimited power.
- Our Lord and Master owns it all, rules it all, and controls it all.
- The Lord My Shepherd guides us, helps us, and remains with us as He cares for us.
- The Most High God is exalted, superior in might and authority over all, and the only one worthy of all our praise.
- He is our Everlasting God, the Beginning and the End, constant and faithful, eternal and unchanging and trustworthy in every way.

Standing in awe of God's power, David declared, "The voice of the LORD is powerful; the voice of the LORD is majestic" (Psalm 29:4). God's promises, sealed with certainty, fueled David with faith that withstood his years of waiting in the wilderness while Saul chased him down. When feelings started to dictate his actions, David could bend his ear to listen to the voice of the Lord. Whether he bore the burden of grief, fear, worry, or guilt, the psalmist leaned into the surety of God's holy Word. His personal reputation mattered less than what others thought about his God. His feelings didn't make him stop trusting the Lord. His hardships didn't push him away from his mighty and merciful maker and sustainer. David trusted God's Word when God's hand didn't seem to be moving in his situation.

Why did he stand on the firm foundation of the words God spoke? Because the Lord's voice was not silenced by his circumstances, manipulated by his surroundings, or snuffed by his struggles or shortcomings. "The voice of the LORD breaks the cedars" (v. 5), fast-growing and hardy trees designed to thrive in various types of soil. "The voice of the LORD twists the oaks and strips the forests bare" (v. 9). The strong trunks of the mighty oak, a symbol of knowledge, bend like soft clay in the hands of God. When David faced his giant and those who persecuted him, he grew weary, frustrated, and afraid. Yet, he continued to sing, "The LORD is enthroned as King forever" (v. 10). Our problems will pass away, but the Lord remains true to His unchanging character forever. Our words will fade away and be forgotten, but the Lord sticks to keeping His promises. "The grass withers and the flowers fall, but the word of our God endures forever" (Isaiah 40:8). David believed this truth wholeheartedly. Lynda lives like she believes every God-breathed word of Scripture.

Like these two faith-warriors, we can hang our hopes on the certainty of the Lord's unchanging and unfailing truth when we're waiting for Him to show us the next step He wants us to take. God gives us all we need to thrive, not just survive, through the wait. As His beloved children, we don't have to be dictated by worry or weighed down by the burdens of our ever-changing emotions. The immeasurable grace of God empowers every breath of our victorious praise through the winding valleys of the wait. When we need answers, courage, strength, or just a moment of peace, God is with us. We may not find our way out of the maze of trials today, but we can trust the One who paves our path with everlasting love and mercy that surpasses our understanding.

INHALE

The LORD gives strength to His people;
the LORD blesses His people with peace.

—PSALM 29:11

EXHALE

Loving Strength-Giver and Peace-Provider, thanks for caring about the details of our lives, for assuring us that you never change, never fail, never let us down.

Please help us remember that your thoughts are not our thoughts and that our understanding is limited by how far we can see.

Empower us spiritually as you give us the confidence to wait like warriors, loving you and others selflessly and sacrificially.

Help us view the wait as a collection of countless opportunities to get to know you more, trust you more, honor you more, and worship you more.

When our flesh feels weak, help us to refrain from apologizing and, instead, to rejoice in the ways our weaknesses magnify your strength.

Forgive us for our uncertainty when we can't see around the bend, Lord. Please help us trust your holy vision, believe your Holy Word, and depend on your Holy Spirit as we walk in victorious praise one day, one moment, one breath at a time.

In Jesus's name, Amen.

- Who inspires your faith as they wait actively and victoriously, even though their struggles don't seem to be ending on this side of eternity?

- How can our faith be strengthened by placing our hope in who God is and what His names tell us about His character?

- How can God's proven faithfulness and the reliability of His promises help us wait like warriors?

Most High God,
your unlimited understanding
is worth trusting in the wait.

12

Purposed Patience

TODAY'S TRUTH

Time cannot deter God's perfect plans.

TODAY'S READING: *Job 38–42*

When I lost my first baby due to a miscarriage, I didn't know God. With no friends in my new city, I fell into a deep depression. I lashed out at my husband and saw no hope for my marriage. I made excuses to avoid work and planned to quit when I regained enough energy to speak to anyone. My boss, Winona, left numerous messages on my phone. *I'm praying for you. When are you coming back to work? Are you okay? I'm on my way over.* She was kidding, right? Nope. She arrived within fifteen minutes, demanded I get ready for work, and gently dragged me out of my self-pity ditch.

The first night I returned to work, we closed the store in silence until I couldn't hold in the sorrow. She cried with me, encouraged me, and assured me that she'd be at my house the next day if I didn't show up to work on time. She never told me to "get over it." She never criticized me for "overreacting, since I wasn't that far along." She never minimized my pain or told me that time would heal my wounds and somehow mend my broken heart. Instead, my boss stood beside me during my grieving process, a loving act which planted the seed for our decades-long friendship.

Winona had a personal relationship with God, while I had mixed emotions and a whole lot of misconceptions about God. I watched her going head-to-head with problem after problem, climbing obstacle after obstacle, trusting her Lord to provide miracle after miracle. She welcomed trials as "endurance training," complete with joyful praise. When she hit a wall of frustration, she would proclaim, "Lord, I know you're trying to strengthen me for something." When the wait pushed her to her limit, when heartaches rose like water behind the gates of a dam, I could hear Winona breathing a prayer. "Can I just catch my breath, Lord?"

When things didn't work out like she'd hoped, my friend clung to the assurance of God's infinite wisdom. She tossed around Winona-isms with a joy-radiating smile that made me wish I could have the faith she had. "We might not understand the what or the why," she said, "but God knows how everything's going to play out." And, "It will all come together right on time—His time, not mine."

Through job loss, financial struggles, and a near foreclosure that dragged on for years, Winona lifted her hands up in total surrender. And as the years passed, I witnessed her walking by a faith more genuine than I'd ever imagined possible. My heart began to soften toward the God I thought was a punisher but learned was a patient and loving provider.

Winona was one of the first people I called when I surrendered my life to Christ. She taught me that following Jesus wouldn't lead to a guarantee of prosperity in worldly things. In the Bible and in Christian history, righteous people struggled. As we live for Christ in this fallen world, righteous people still struggle. Some suffering will end on this side of eternity, but some will not. When I begin to allow weariness to warp my thinking on suffering, I take a closer look at Winona's life and remember Job.

Scripture introduces us to Job, who was "blameless and upright; he feared God and shunned evil" (Job 1:1). "He was the greatest man among all the people of the East" (v. 3), faithful husband, devoted father, kind employer.

And did we mention he was wealthy? Satan mocked Job, claiming he was only righteous because God "put a hedge around him" and "blessed the work of his hands" (v. 10). Of course Job could remain a righteous and grateful lover of God while life rolled by smoothly. But what if his journey hit a few snags?

Satan set a target on Job's back, *convinced* Job would turn away from God if things stopped going his way. "He will surely curse you to your face," the Father of Lies said to God (v. 11).

The devil murdered Job's children and caused his financial devastation. Overcome with grief, Job allowed himself to process his emotions. But he knew God was the maker and giver of all good things when he said, "The LORD gave and the LORD has taken away; may the name of the LORD be praised" (v. 21); Job understood that everything he had was on loan, entrusted to him for a season.

Job's surrender doesn't mean he didn't care about his losses. When he tore his robes and shaved his head, Job demonstrated his faith in God's approachability and compassion. He knew the Lord could handle his raw honesty as he grieved. He knew God was completely good and faithful and just, even when life seemed totally unfair and circumstances felt unbearable. Job's confidence in God's trustworthiness led him to fall to the ground in worship. "In all this, Job did not sin by charging God with wrongdoing" (v. 22).

And yet his intense spiritual battle wasn't over. As time went on, Satan "afflicted Job with painful sores from the soles of his feet to the crown of his head" (Job 2:7). After losing his children, his wealth, and his health, Job could have blamed God and questioned His goodness. Instead, Job's response mirrored the testimony I witnessed in Winona's life. Knowing he had nothing that was not first given to him by the Lord, Job said, "Shall we accept good from God, and not trouble?" (v. 10).

This mighty man of faith didn't deny his suffering or minimize the severity of his pain. He continued to honor God, even as his wife and friends badgered him with their unwanted opinions. He trusted, even when God was silent. Even when God's plan didn't make sense, even when God's pace seemed unreasonable, Job waited for God with courageous confidence. Finally, "the LORD spoke to Job out of the storm" (Job 38:1). While God didn't stop Job's heartache or rescue him from his pain in that instant, He did something that would deepen Job's faith, something that still encourages others toward enduring faith. In the midst of Job's troubles, God affirmed the sufficiency of His grandness, His trustworthiness, and His faithfulness as creator and sustainer of all. Once Job turned his eyes away from his ever-changing circumstances and toward his never-changing Lord, he developed an eternal perspective. He said, "I know that you can do all things; no purpose of yours can be thwarted" (Job 42:2). Hallelujah!

Trials and heartache can tempt us to gripe and lash out at God and others. As we wait for the Lord to work things out, we may feel bombarded by relentless storms. Even when we remember that God is refining our hearts and sculpting our character through our circumstances and our relationships, we can doubt, fear, and be tempted to give up. Some heartaches and seasons of waiting feel impossible to bear, which is why the Lord blesses us with communion with His people and with Him—our loving and limitless Father.

The Lord takes His time, not to punish us but to prepare us for His bigger-than-our-lives and ever-prevailing plans. He won't require us to wait one second more than we need. With loving patience, He ensures our victory in Him and affirms His plans were already set into motion before one of our days came to be.

INHALE

I know that you can do all things;
no purpose of yours can be thwarted.
—JOB 42:2

EXHALE

Good and caring Shepherd, we adore you. Thanks for proclaiming your majesty, for affirming you are in control no matter what's going on around us. Giver of all good things, thanks for caring for us perfectly.

Please help us loosen our grip on the things of this world. Give us the courage to submit to your timetable and trust your heart to give and take away as you see fit. Help us surrender to you, our faithful Father and compassionate Friend, as we learn to open ourselves up to your intimate love.

Give us the wisdom and strength we need to live for you, mighty Jesus, fully dependent on the reliability of your faithfulness. Help us to be confident that your plan and pace are perfect, that your purposes will prevail, even when the emotions are hard to process and your ways seem impossible to understand.

Please, Lord, give us endurance as we accept that the details of our lives are a small part of your greater purpose.

In Jesus's name, Amen.

- When have you struggled to let go of something or someone, and had a hard time processing your feelings with the Lord?

- In what situation or situations are you currently feeling the need for God to give you some breathing room or a break in the storm?

- What characteristics of God help you trust His purpose and empower you to persevere when the trials seem relentless and the wait feels endless?

Merciful Maker,
your faithfulness endures longer
than our wait can last.
Hallelujah!

13

Going with the Flow

Complications foiling our well-laid plans can foster impatience, frustration, anxiety, and plain ol' grumpiness. Usually I travel with cheerleading pom-poms and a glass-half-full perspective. When situations take a turn for the worse, I scour the skies for clouds with silver linings. When unexpected obstacles toss a wrench into perfectly organized plans, my family knows the drill. *Go with the flow. God is faithful. We'll have fun, fun, fun . . . as long as we trust the Lord and stick together.* Of course, some circumstances can push me close to the barely-holding-it-together edge.

When Xavier was young, my frugal husband surprised us with a too-good-to-be-true vacation deal that included three destinations. All we had to do was pay travel expenses and redeem all three vacations within three years. I praised God and scheduled the first trip to the nearest destination. The following year, we soaked up the Lord's blessings as we enjoyed the sand and sun of the tropics. Then we started saving vacation time and funds for the last trip, excited to experience the grand finale of our package deal. As we neared the three-year mark, all of our plans fell into place. *Passports? Check. Packing? Double check. Covered in prayer? Triple check. Cancun, here we come.*

My Spanish came in handy when we arrived at the airport. I found a taxi while Alan gathered our luggage. Climbing into the cab with my family, I thanked God for our safe travels and greeted the driver.

The cabby's brows gathered when I told him the name of our hotel. "Are you sure?"

Xavier piped up. "Are we close? I'm hungry."

Our driver nodded. "Oh, we're close." He navigated through the airport traffic and zipped past a few fancy resorts and extravagant hotels.

Praising the Lord for the ways He'd worked over the last three years, I anticipated the elegance of the suite reserved for us on the golf course. When we turned off the main road, my mom-radar flashed. We snaked down a narrow, winding street. I glanced at my husband when the driver parked in front of a structure that looked more like a condemned building than a five-star resort. Gulp. *Lord . . . uh . . .* Gulp.

We had nowhere else to go, so we checked in. Alan lugged our bags to the broken elevator. "Go with the flow?"

"I'm sure they're going to fix the elevator," I said. I followed my guys up three flights of stairs. *Lord, help us.* Plastering a smile on my face wasn't as easy when we rounded the corner and started toward the second floor. "I'm sure the rooms are beautiful. Remember the pictures?"

When we entered the musty room, Alan tossed our bags on the floor. It didn't take long to figure out that the air conditioner, the full-sized refrigerator, and the phone didn't work.

Alan looked at me. "I'm so sorry," he said.

Beads of sweat slipped down my temple. Placing my hand on my hard-working husband's arm, I inhaled the muggy air and exhaled another prayer. *Help me to be grateful, Lord.* I mustered up my best chipper voice and said, "Let's get into our swimsuits. I'll change our room while you guys hang out at the pool."

When Alan picked up our large, red duffel bag, I noticed four dime-sized roaches had been crushed into the tile floor. "Nope. Nope. Nope," I said, picking Xavier up. "We're out of here."

With my family camped out in the lobby, I bit my tongue when the front desk manager hustled me out of twenty bucks for a phone fee. *Lord, please forgive me for what I really want to say to this guy.* I called the travel agency's toll-free number. I took one prayer-breath after another while spending over four hours waiting for the kind representative to find us a suitable replacement hotel.

Raising my hand high, I hung up. "Thank you, Lord!" I arranged for a taxi to drive us across town. The manager at our new resort presented us with a voucher for a free meal at the on-site restaurant. He commended us for having "such grateful attitudes after such an ordeal."

"Oh, there were times I was praying through clenched teeth." I laughed. "But I knew God would take care of us."

When we entered the air-conditioned room, I blinked back thankful tears. The bright colors, plush furniture, and private beach just outside the living area's sliding door was more than I had asked for and way more than I expected. *Lord, thanks for being so good to us, so good.*

Later, I watched my guys splashing in the pool. I praised God for His overflowing faithfulness. Our perfect vacation did not go as we planned. One obstacle after another tried my patience. But as the experience dragged on and on and on, we did our best to witness to those who watched the ways we dealt with our difficulties while trusting God.

It's not easy to abstain from griping when inconvenienced. It's even harder to keep calm when our situations tilt toward painful and overwhelming. If anyone could find a reason to complain about his circumstances, it would be the apostle Paul.

People didn't want to forget his past life as a persecutor of the church, so he had a tough time being accepted as he preached about Jesus, until Barnabas vouched for him (Acts 9:26–28). He had to work harder and was imprisoned "more frequently" and "flogged more severely" than his fellow servants of Christ (2 Corinthians 11:23). Paul endured being beaten with rods, pelted with stones, and shipwrecked three times. He lived on the lam in constant danger; he "labored and toiled," often going without sleep or food. "Besides everything else," Paul bore the "pressure" of his "concern for all the churches" (v. 28). He cared deeply for those who rejected him because they were rejecting Christ. Bombarded with suffering and scarred by ongoing trials, Paul could have fallen into discouragement and doubt. Instead, Paul remained loyal to Jesus. In Philippians 4:4, he instructs us to "rejoice in the Lord *always*." He then seems to realize how hard that sounds, so he repeats himself. "I will say it again: Rejoice!"

We don't have to *enjoy* suffering or *have fun* facing our problems in order to rejoice in the peace of God's presence. Knowing the Lord remains near us can empower us to maintain a gentle and joyful spirit no matter what our circumstances. As we rely on our ongoing and intimate communication with God, His peace prevails . . . even when everything else goes wrong. When we insist on life going according to our plans, we may block ourselves from God's better-than-our-best blessings. Instead, we can go with the flow as God wraps us in grace and carries us through each unexpected detour in our wild adventure through the wait.

INHALE

Do not be anxious about anything,
but in every situation, by prayer and petition,
with thanksgiving, present your requests to God.
—PHILIPPIANS 4:6

EXHALE

Wise Counselor, you are worthy of all our praise. Please forgive us for the times we've placed our trust in the things of this world, in people who cannot save us, redeem us, or change our hearts. Forgive us for the times we've allowed our joy to be robbed by our circumstances.

Please continue to affirm your presence through our day-to-day living as we place our hope in you, the Maker of the heavens, the earth, the sea, and everything in them.

Only you, Lord, remain faithful forever. Hallelujah!

Thanks for lifting us up when we're bowed down. Thanks for providing for us and freeing us from all that binds us and keeps us from the freedom you offer. Thanks for loving us as we are and loving us enough to invest in making us more like you. When situations get rough, help us remember you're watching over us, sustaining us, and protecting us, Lord.

Please help us reflect your character in the ways we respond to trials.

Please anchor our joy and peace in the surety of your ongoing presence and faithfulness as we praise you all the days of our lives.

In Jesus's name, Amen.

- Why is it often difficult to remain flexible when our plans don't go as we hope?

- How can communicating with God through Bible study and prayer increase our trust in His faithfulness?

- What situation do you need to release so you can go with God's flow?

Lord of Peace,
help us remember you reign over all circumstances,
all obstacles, all detours, and all delays.

14

In the Presence of Power

TODAY'S TRUTH

As we acknowledge the constant presence of God,
we can walk and wait in the power of God.

TODAY'S READING: *Mark 4:35–41*

As I prepared to pack up, move to Seattle, and serve as a live-in caregiver for my mom after her bone marrow transplant, I asked our church family to keep us on the ongoing prayer list. One of our senior couples, Mr. Charles and Ms. June, approached me after service on my last Sunday in California. After they prayed for me, Mr. Charles handed me a framed poem by an anonymous writer entitled, "What Cancer Cannot Do." He offered a word of encouragement, sharing why the poem inspired him. He'd been battling cancer for over a decade, without much of a break.

If you or someone you love has endured physical suffering, you know: constant fighting requires an incredible amount of energy and can take a draining toll on a person's body and mind. It's easy to allow the disease or disability to run things, to feel helpless and defeated. But that was definitely not the case with Mr. Charles or Ms. June.

They both experienced physical pain daily. They could have bowed down under discouragement, but instead they encouraged others. Their faith remained vibrant because God himself served as their Power Source. Because of that, they could give without fear of running out of resources.

Mr. Charles used social media to share God's truth and love. Each post affirmed that suffering could not smother his joy in Christ. When Mr. Charles entered a room, no matter how severe his pain levels, strangers became friends as he greeted them with a genuine toothy grin and wrapped them in a big ol' love-of-Jesus hug. And when Mr. Charles's health took a turn for the worse, visitors left the hospital feeling inspired to persevere and praise the Lord. He used the opportunity to share the gospel one more time, encourage hearts one more time, point to Jesus one more time. Mr. Charles's body withered, but his faith blossomed.

Cancer couldn't cripple Mr. Charles's ability to love, because he loved out of the overflow of God's love for him. Cancer couldn't shatter his hope, because he placed his hope in Christ—the Lord and Savior of the world. Cancer couldn't corrode his faith, because the very source of his faith was Jesus. Cancer couldn't silence his courage, invade his soul, or steal his eternal life because he remained anchored in the unchanging and infallible Word of God. Cancer could never conquer Mr. Charles's spirit, because this mighty man of God was empowered by the Holy Spirit. Hallelujah!

Even the weariest heart can be refreshed while waiting for God by living each day in the limitless power of the One True God, the Triune God, the Father-Son-and-Holy-Spirit God. Joy and peace don't depend on circumstances when a soul is nourished by the transforming power of the Maker and Sustainer of all. Like Mr. Charles, we can count on the life-giving power of Jesus—who is fully man and fully God, the Lord and Savior of the world, the Beginning and the End, the Alpha and the Omega.

The twelve disciples knew the regenerating power of the Messiah firsthand, but even they needed reminders of how vital it was to abide in His intimate presence. After a full day of teaching, Jesus took some time with the disciples. They left the crowds behind and set out on the Sea of Galilee in a boat. The evening current lulled some to sleep. Even the Lord enjoyed a deep slumber as the boat drifted further from the shore. Suddenly, "a furious squall came up, and the waves broke over the boat, so that it was nearly swamped" (Mark 4:37). Cold water soaked the disciples' clothes and threatened to sink the boat. In that moment, fear rendered them hopeless. The disciples seemed to forget all they knew about Jesus, all they'd seen Him do, all they'd heard Him promise.

"The disciples woke him and said to him, 'Teacher, don't you care if we drown?'" (v. 38). I can't even tally the number of times I've cried out to the Lord in a similar fashion. Don't you care, Lord? Doesn't it bother you when I'm hurting, when the path you set before me leads me straight into turmoil? Don't you care that I'm afraid?

How many times did the Lord assure the disciples that He was in control, that He was sovereign and good, that He was with them no matter how wild life's storms raged? Still, the disciples fretted and doubted the Lord's care.

Yet Jesus didn't ignore their desperate cries. "He got up, rebuked the wind and said to the waves, 'Quiet! Be still!' Then the wind died down and it was completely calm" (v. 39). With His words, the Messiah calmed the wind and waves and the tender hearts of the trembling disciples. By His words, He affirmed the greatness of His majesty. Who else but the Maker of all could control it all? Who else but God could quiet a fierce storm with a few syllables? Quiet. Be still. Jesus spoke to the wind and waves, but He could have been talking to the disciples.

"He said to the disciples, 'Why are you so afraid? Do you still have no faith?'" (v. 40). I don't think he was shaming the disciples. Rather, I hear the Lord's heart breaking: *What do I have to do to make you trust Me, believe Me, rest in Me?*

After all the disciples had witnessed, after the Messiah had changed their lives, they still resorted to fear and doubt when faced with the unexpected.

I'd like to say I've never questioned the Lord like the disciples. I'd like to say I've never responded to difficult situations with trembling hands, afraid to allow God to give and take away as He deems necessary. But it's not always easy to remember God sifts all our circumstances through His grace, strengthening us, preparing us, transforming us as He reveals himself to us.

Though He won't always quiet our storms, Jesus will always quiet our hearts while He remains close and in control. Though He won't always prevent our ships from sinking . . . our friends from dying, our children from wandering, our health from declining, our businesses from failing, our creditors from calling . . . Jesus will hear our prayers, welcome our honest cries for help, and assure us of the power of His ongoing presence.

Like Mr. Charles and his widow, Ms. June, we can follow Jesus through the valleys and climb the Meantime Mountains He's prepared for us. Like the disciples, when the waves drench us, we can call on Jesus for mercy, admit our fears, confess our doubt . . . and trust Him to make the power of His presence known.

Jesus's supremacy never weakens. His promises never fail. His loving presence never, ever leaves us. We can worship the Lord and give Him all the glory as we draw nearer to Him and proclaim His storm-stilling, spirit-refreshing, and heart-changing power.

INHALE

Jesus is the same yesterday
and today and forever.
—HEBREWS 13:8

EXHALE

Supreme Lord of Lords, thanks for enabling us to live in the power of your ongoing presence. Please help us hear your heartbeat when the darkness threatens to obscure our vision and smother our hopes.

When we're feeling tossed back and forth by fierce winds, when our knees tremble and our souls are downcast, please reassure us with your unchanging truth and reminders of who you are and all you've done. When we are afraid, help us trust in you.

Empower us to praise you, to place our hope in You, and to be rejuvenated by the comfort You've given us in and through all circumstances. Please reveal yourself to us and make us new with confident and courageous faith.

Help us list the countless ways you've proven yourself faithful, especially when we're facing fear, discouragement, and doubt. Help us to be honest with you, Lord, trusting you can handle our truth and help us with our unbelief.

Help us look beyond our own misery to serve others in love and share you with boldness, until the day you call us home.

In Jesus's name, Amen.

- How do you acknowledge God's constant presence?

- How can communing with the Lord continually change the way we face waiting seasons that feel endless and impossible to endure?

- Why can you trust the Lord when you or a loved one are waiting for God to move in a situation and relief does not seem to be coming on this side of eternity?

*Our Lord and Refuge, thanks for being stable
no matter how shaky our circumstances.*

15

The Hope of Being Heard

TODAY'S TRUTH

God's promise to hear us
is the stronghold of our hope.

TODAY'S READING: *Psalm 18*

With an aching heart, I walked into the room filled with laughter and everything-pink decorations. A group of us had gathered to support our friend with prayer and commitments to be by her side during the long healing journey ahead. Since she couldn't alter God's plan or determine His pace, Yami wanted to control at least one thing in her battle with breast cancer. So, before the side effects of chemotherapy kicked in, we scheduled the hair-cutting party. Both of her beautiful daughters chopped off their long and lovely locks. Her supportive husband shaved his head. Another friend cut off over ten inches of curl.

Yami's family supported her, but couldn't possibly be with her every second of the day. By God's grace, the women of God she called friends organized meals and scheduled home visits. We even arranged to be with her during treatments. One of our friends brought enough food to share with nurses and other patients who felt like eating. When Yami's family members couldn't be with her during appointments, her praying friends stepped up to surround her with love.

The Lord knows that cancer affects everyone who loves the patient, and He has given us two priceless gifts to strengthen us through the seemingly endless wait—caring community and intercessory prayer. The sisters in Christ who surrounded Yami during the pink party remained by her side through every dip, detour, and delay of her fight. Watching these women loving one another inspired me to love better. When I joined these ladies to support Yami and her family, I experienced community on a deeper level than I ever had before. I learned how to let others support me as I offered them help. And during the rough patches, I learned how helpless we all were without Jesus.

Although my own battle with chronic pain hindered my ability to offer physical support, I volunteered to be Yami's prayer partner. During one of our visits, she showed me some of the artwork she'd created when she needed to fix her eyes on Jesus. I encouraged her as she drew cartoon images with hope-messages and Scripture to share with others; however, the Lord used her to encourage me even more. Late one night, as I struggled through another bout with chronic pain, my phone rang. I recognized my friend's number. Breathing a prayer for strength, I pushed myself out of my recliner and winced as my back spasms increased. I met my husband's concerned gaze. "It's Yami," I said.

He nodded. "Are you okay?"

I shrugged, smiled weakly, answered the phone, and headed to the bedroom. Certain that the late call would be a prayer request, I was prepared to listen before inviting her to come before the Lord in prayer. Instead, Yami greeted me with uncontrollable sobs. Her recent treatment had triggered random stretches of high-level pain without relief. The meds didn't work. The home therapy didn't work. Nothing seemed to help her when the deep aching started. *What am I supposed to do, Lord?* I couldn't take away her pain. I couldn't shorten her journey. I couldn't assure her that the pain would subside. As we both wept, the minutes rolled by. Still, I couldn't muster up the right words to reassure my hurting friend. Nothing. When her sobs escalated into wails, I choked out a whispered prayer. "Jesus . . . Jesus . . . Jesus."

I repeated the prayer with a surefire hope of being heard until the Lord eased me into His peace. "Jesus . . . Jesus . . . Jesus." As I continued calling out to our eternal Prince of Peace, Yami's cries slowed to whimpers and sniffles. Her breathing grew heavier and heavier.

Closing my eyes, I pressed my cheek into my now-damp pillow. "Jesus . . . Jesus . . . Jesus."

Her husband's whisper startled me. "She's asleep," he said. "We'll call you tomorrow."

Hanging up, I thanked the Lord for hearing our prayers, especially the silent supplications that slipped down our cheeks. Wrapped in God's peace, I continued worshipping Him with devotion that could have matched the psalmist David's prayer-like songs of praise. "I love you, LORD, my strength" (Psalm 18:1).

After experiencing the Lord's timely care, David declared, "The LORD is my rock, my fortress and my deliverer; my God is my rock, in whom I take refuge, my shield and the horn of my salvation, my stronghold" (vv. 2–3). David's intimate way of addressing the Lord assures us of His immediate availability when we call on Him. David spoke directly to God then burst into worshipful declarations of God's personal connection with His children. We can replicate his approach to communing with our maker and sustainer.

David knew what it was like to fear for his life: "The cords of death entangled me; the torrents of destruction overwhelmed me. The cords of the grave coiled around me; the snares of death confronted me" (vv. 4–5). No matter how our lives are threatened—physically, emotionally, spiritually—like David, we can be certain God hears our sobs and our silent cries. Like the psalmist, we can sing, "In my distress I called to the LORD; I cried to my God for help. . . . My cry came before him, into his ears" (v. 6). Whether we need strength to face a physical adversary like David or an illness like Yami, God is the Hope-Giver who empowers us to persevere through the longest and darkest battles in life.

God's children can declare what we know to be true, even in the middle of our pain-filled wait. We can sing about the Lord's proven faithfulness in Scripture, in the lives of others, and in our lives. We can join David and proclaim, "You, LORD, keep my lamp burning; my God turns my darkness into light" (v. 28). Hallelujah!

We can do nothing without the life-giving, soul-restoring, heart-transforming Good Shepherd—the Lord Almighty—who guides and provides for us. David acknowledges this truth as he cries out with bold resolve and praises God for who He is and all He's able to do. The psalmist speaks to the Lord then testifies about Him: "With your help I can advance against a troop; with my God I can scale a wall. As for God, his way is perfect: The LORD's word is flawless; he shields all who take refuge in him" (vv. 29–30).

Notice that David never tries to take credit for God's mighty works or power. Though David is the anointed, soon-to-be king, he wears his weaknesses like a golden badge of honor and accepts his dependence on the Lord. "It is God who arms me with strength and keeps my way secure" (v. 32). David speaks with sturdy hope firmly established in the Lord's irrevocable love for him.

We, too, can rest in God's constant presence with that same assurance binding us to a durable faith. With thankful certainty, we can know God hears every prayer, even those that slip down our cheeks as tears. Our voices will reach the ears and the heart of God . . . whether those pleas are spoken, silent . . . or desperate sobs hidden in the echo of His name, as we whisper, "Jesus. Jesus. Jesus."

INHALE

In my distress I called to the LORD;
I cried to my God for help.
From his temple he heard my voice;
my cry came before him, into his ears.

—PSALM 18:6

EXHALE

*Hearer of Our Heart Cries, thanks for blessing us with the assurance
of your reliable character. Thanks for giving us the ability to praise you,
to remember all you've done, and to be grateful for all you're able to
accomplish.*

*When we feel unheard, please assure us that you are always
good and always listening. When we feel alone, please affirm your
continuous presence. When fear or doubt overwhelms us, please remind
us that you are sovereign and faithful, now and forever.*

*Help us nestle into the knowledge of who we are in light of who
you are, Good Shepherd. When we can't understand the why of our
situations or figure out the how of the road ahead, please let your mercy
overflow and nurture a worshipful attitude in us.*

*When we can't find the words to pray either for ourselves or to
encourage others, help us remember you know our needs and are already
working. Please help us find comfort in knowing your love endures and
your strength replenishes us as we recognize the power in your name.*

In Jesus's name, Amen.

- What God-breathed words of Scripture have given you
  strength, comfort, peace, and hope when you couldn't
  find the words to pray?

- What situation in your life is requiring you to call on
  Jesus in prayer and simply trust Him to meet your needs?

- Who has God placed in your life to grieve with you and encourage you in the wait, and who do you grieve with and encourage in their wait? (If you're feeling alone, you can ask God to guide you to a prayerful community. You can also experience loving encouragement when you join my blog family at www.xedixon.com.)

Good Father,
thanks for hearing our cries.

16

God's Ever-Flowing Comfort

TODAY'S TRUTH

God's ever-flowing comfort
fuels our power in the wait.

TODAY'S READING: *2 Corinthians 1:3–7*

Shelly Jean Beach lives with post-traumatic stress disorder caused by years of suffering from various degrees of physical, emotional, and mental trauma. She endures excruciating pain, debilitating fatigue and headaches, and a host of other issues due to multiple sclerosis, which only adds to her struggles with PTSD. Yet, for years she has served as a caregiver, even while needing caregiving herself. Her challenges increased after she met Wanda Sanchez, a woman who struggled with C-PTSD caused by abuse and severe childhood neglect.

With a heart overflowing with love for Jesus and people, Shelly invited Wanda to move in with her family. The move was good for Wanda, who underwent successful trauma treatment and became stronger over time. And it was good for Shelly, as Wanda encouraged her to take better care of herself. But when it became apparent that Wanda was intent on committing suicide, Shelly became anxious. What if her friend succeeded? "I lost everyone I'd taken care of in the past," she said. "I couldn't help but worry."

Together, they recognized that the strain of codependence had taken them to an unhealthy place. The friends turned to the Lord and worked out a system to help both of them feel better about their time apart. "I had to step back and let God do what only He could do as Wanda healed physically, emotionally, and spiritually, and I learned to trust Him in new ways," said Shelly.

As she and Wanda continued to grow closer to God and to each other, it was hard for Shelly not to feel overly responsible or even totally responsible for her friend. "I have innate smothering instincts," said Shelly. "As a mom—my ultimate caregiving assignment—I thought I needed to conform my kids to *my own* image." She had to remember that she couldn't change them; only the Holy Spirit could do that. Shelly confesses that she's still learning that lesson in her relationship with Wanda. "No one should have to go through what Wanda went through." Shelly's voice cracked. "I wanted to pour into her. It was important to me."

Shelly learned firsthand that compassion can become exhausting when we try to do God's job. "It's important to be able to sit back and trust God, to trust her, to let the two of them have their own relationship. Wanda and God. Me and God. *Then*, us and God." Waiting for God can be maddening. We feel helpless, unable to fix situations or protect people from hurt. But the Holy Spirit helps us trust He's working, even when we're not working.

Shelly and Wanda now rely on God's power as they serve others who suffer from PTSD. The friends coauthored *Love Letters from the Edge*, a devotional for people who question God while suffering and waiting for Him to move in their situation. As they penned each letter to God, expressing their heartache with raw honesty, they used Scripture to create letters from God in response. They also founded PTSD Perspectives (ptsd perspectives.org) and continue offering support and resources to those suffering from PTSD and the people who care for them.

The apostle Paul could have easily struggled with codependency and PTSD. Instead, he lived dependent on and surrendered to Christ as he rejoiced in his weaknesses. Paul knew his power as a servant of God came *from* God, the one who saved him and the only one who could save other people. In his second letter to the church of Corinth, Paul modeled the life of Christ by allowing his selfless suffering to result in the generous giving of himself to benefit others. He opens the letter with a moment of worship: "Praise be to the God and Father of our Lord Jesus Christ, the Father of compassion and the God of all comfort, who comforts us in all our troubles, *so that* we can comfort those in any trouble with the comfort we ourselves receive from God" (2 Corinthians 1:3–4, emphasis mine).

When we're having a hard time accepting God's plan and pace for ourselves and our hurting loved ones, we can turn to Jesus, our High Priest. He is the only one who can truly "empathize with our weaknesses" (Hebrews 4:15). God in the flesh— Jesus—endured physical, emotional, mental, and spiritual pain, especially the torment of dying on the cross, separated from the Father, in order to pay the debt for our sins. Christ chose to know the weakness and limitations of the flesh. He invites us to approach Him with complete reliance in His ability to understand our most intimate needs. And He invites us to bring our hurting friends to Him through intercessory prayer. "Let us then approach God's throne of grace with confidence, so that we may receive mercy and find grace to help us in our time of need" (v. 16). He's the only one who can rescue us and the people we love.

As we deepen our relationships with God and trust Him through our trials, His ever-flowing comfort gives us peace and also strengthens us to persevere with bold faith as we rely on Him (2 Corinthians 1:5–7). He'll come alongside us and use our past experiences to equip us for serving others by sharing how

He helped us. He'll empower us to use the gifts He's entrusted to us and the experiences He's brought us through to offer encouragement and resources to people in need. The Lord knows we may need help from doctors or counselors, and often medication too, when dealing with physical, mental, and emotional affliction. Needing medical professionals and the resources they provide does not show a lack of faith, and it doesn't minimize or replace our need for God. Ultimately, we're all dependent on Christ, the only one who can save us, change us, make us new, and lead us to the resources and professional help we need. God will give us and those we care about the comfort we need to be strong in Him. Only God can fuel us with power to comfort others from His ever-flowing love and compassion in our lives.

INHALE

For our light and momentary troubles
are achieving for us an eternal glory
that far outweighs them all.
—2 CORINTHIANS 4:17

EXHALE

Lord, thanks for blessing us with soul-refreshing peace and for affirming you never waste our time or our experiences.

When relief seems unlikely on this side of eternity, please help us embrace our afflictions with confidence in your all-knowing and purpose-driven goodness. Fuel us with your strength-giving comfort so we can serve you with gladness. Help us make the most of every opportunity to share how you've worked in and through our longest and hardest seasons in life.

Please help us approach your throne of grace with bold personal and intercessory prayers. Help us live with our palms, our hearts, and our minds wide open, ready and willing to invite you to give and take away as you see fit.

When hardships seem to be unending, please give us grace for the moment, Lord. Supply us with all we need to trust you with each step on the path you've prepared for us and those we love.
In Jesus's name, Amen.

- How does witnessing others serving in the midst of their wait—while still relying on the Lord to sustain them day by day—help deepen your faith?

- In what situation are you expecting God to remain faithful even when your situation isn't turning out as you'd hoped?

- Describe a time when you tried to do God's job in the life of a hurting loved one or someone tried to help you by trying to do the Holy Spirit's work in you. How does knowing we're not responsible for changing one another help you trust God's plan and pace during trials or relational conflicts?

Father of compassion
and God of all comfort,
please comfort us
with your constant presence.

17

The One and Only

TODAY'S TRUTH

*Only God can sustain
us in the wait.*

TODAY'S READING: *Isaiah 46*

When she turned twenty-six, Aurora surrendered her life to Christ and embraced the freedom and joy of being a new creation. She could hardly wait to serve the Lord who saved her. But one week after her life-changing decision, her husband served her with divorce papers.

Though thrust into a new world she hadn't planned on being a part of, Aurora kept serving the Lord and moved forward. No looking back. Surely God would bless her with a good husband as she followed His leading. Surely He wouldn't let her dream die . . . would He?

As she ticked the days off the calendar year after year, her confidence began to flicker with fear, doubt, insecurity, and anger. Why wouldn't God give her a husband? He knew her desires for a family. She was ready. What was taking the Lord so long?

When she turned thirty, she jumped into a relationship with Mr. Right Now. She stayed in that relationship with Mr. Won't Commit for five years. She wanted more. She wanted marriage. But he had grown content with being Mr. Still Single.

Aurora felt the Lord nudging her to end the relationship, but feared her beau was Mr. Last Chance. She waited, hoping God would change his heart. Instead, God moved Mr. Not-the-One hundreds of miles away.

Grieving at thirty-five, Aurora doused her depression with busyness. Her heart-cries spilled out when she wasn't consciously trying to appear content. Why wouldn't God relent? When would He give her the Promised-Land life she knew He could provide?

Aurora trudged toward the summit of the Big 4-0. She adjusted her happy-mask and forced herself to face the idea that she may not get her dreams fulfilled.

Sick . . . and tired . . . of wanting and waiting, Aurora asked God to help her surrender the desires of her broken heart. Why couldn't she just move on? She knew Jesus refers to himself as "the bridegroom," symbolizing the intimate relationship between God and His people. If she believed His identity as God in the flesh, why wasn't Jesus enough for her? The question challenged her faith. Did she truly believe God? Did she pray and live like she believed God?

After some honest reflection, the Lord revealed her idolatry and wrong motives in serving and in prayer. For years, she'd desired a relationship with a man she could call her spouse . . . *more than* she'd yearned for a deeper relationship with God. She compared herself to others, coveting the status of being a wife. She filled her calendar with acts of service to keep herself busy and distracted, leaving herself minimal time to seek the Lord or simply worship Him. Confessing her sins, Aurora repented and asked God to help her live to glorify Him. "Marriage wasn't a prize I needed to obtain," she said. "Married or single, I should want Jesus more than anything or anyone."

With purified motives, Aurora no longer consumed herself with her marital status. She stopped badgering God with doubt-filled prayers while waiting for Him to reward her faithful service with a husband. She served because she wanted to express her love for Him. She spent time with Jesus because He was important to her. Although she still experienced tough times, her faith flourished as she began worshipping the Lord in the deepest canyons of the wait. For the first time in years, Aurora truly wanted God's will to be done, even if it meant she would remain single. She pursued Jesus with persevering faith, loving Him, worshipping Him, and trusting Him through every season . . . even those she didn't want to go through. After she released her grip on what she felt she had to have, God was able to place what she needed into her life.

When Aurora met the man the Lord had been preparing to love her, she was ready to love him in a healthy and holy way.

The week before the wedding, after so many Saturday nights spent *feeling alone* with Jesus, Aurora enjoyed one more Saturday night *being alone* with Jesus. She wept and thanked Him for her extended season of singleness. She praised Him for each year of preparation He knew she needed before saying *I do* at the age of forty-five. After eighteen years of chasing idols—in her case, marriage status and completeness in a spouse—Aurora realized only God could fill her deepest needs. From that day on, she vowed to release her grip on anything and anyone she wanted more than Jesus.

Most of us can relate to Aurora's desire to see her dreams realized and to feeling let down when God doesn't do what we want, give us what we think we need, or move in ways that make us feel better. And most of us have been consumed with idols— things or people we place before God. But, eventually, most of us learn nothing and nobody can satisfy us like God does.

We're not the first of God's people to struggle with idolatry. The prophet Isaiah served as the Lord's mouthpiece to the Israelites. In Isaiah 46, he referred to their man-created idols as "a burden for the weary" (v. 1) that led to their enslavement. Isaiah wanted the people to realize the futility of putting anything in

God's place: a god should be able to carry our burdens, not be a burden that must be carried.

Our Creator knew us before we were born and will be with us through every day He's ordained for us. "I have made you and I will carry you; I will sustain you and I will rescue you," God said to the Israelites (v. 4). No idol can do that. "With whom will you compare me or count me equal? To whom will you liken me that we may be compared?" (v. 5). Oh, how our loving Lord is grieved when we dishonor Him by placing anything or anyone before Him—as if He could possibly be replaced. God has no equal! He is the one and only God. He made us. He supports us and bears our burdens. God holds us up, keeps us going, provides for us. He preserves us, bolsters us in power, and comforts us. Nothing and no person in this world can do what God can do . . . what God has done . . . for us.

When we limit our desires to the things of this world, we're hindered by our own limitations as created beings. Every idol we try to set up in our hearts can only fail us. No matter what happens in the wait, no matter what we're longing for, the Lord Almighty will give us more than enough to persevere. He will be more than enough, because He is the only one who is enough, the one and only true God. The time God provides for us is precious and purposed for His glory. As we fall deeper in love with Jesus, He can give us an eternal perspective. The Holy Spirit can empower us to obey because we want His plan to prevail. Our loving Father can help us trust His perfectly timed pace. To God be the glory, the honor, and the praise!

INHALE

> For I am the LORD your God
> who takes hold of your right hand and says to you,
> Do not fear; I will help you.
> —ISAIAH 41:13

EXHALE

Father God, thanks for pursuing us, for watching over us, and for loving us while we practice keeping you first in our lives.

Please keep our minds focused on you and our hearts devoted to pleasing you and spending time with you above all else and everyone else.

Forgive us for seeking security in the created things of this world, in the created ones instead of you, our Creator. Help us trust in your unfailing love through the days you've ordained for us, no matter how long we're traveling through the waiting seasons in life. Make our faith flourish as we rely on the certainty of your goodness and faithfulness, whether we're waiting for a dream to be reached or a promise to be fulfilled.

And please help us want you more than we want anything or anyone else.

In Jesus's name, Amen.

- What created things or people have you relied on more than God, been reluctant to release to God, or felt tempted to place before God?

- Describe a time when you had to let something or someone go so the Lord could work in and through the wait He ordained for you.

- How can wanting Jesus more than anything or anyone else help you thrive in the waiting seasons He's planned for your life?

Holy God,
there is none like you!

—97—

18

Praying in God's Presence

TODAY'S TRUTH

God hears our prayers and
will stay with us through the wait.

TODAY'S READING: *Exodus 3:1–21*

James Banks seemed thoroughly prepared to deal with intense spiritual attack. He served as a pastor for over thirty years; he'd read through the Word of God every year for a quarter of a century; he'd counseled families through incredible trials. James did his best to stay in prayer and point others to Jesus, including parents with prodigals. But when the enemy attacked his own children and his dreams for his family seemed shattered, the cost got personal. James found himself fighting depression. Thankfully, he didn't stay there. Years later, James reflected on a defining moment in his journey. "God prompted me to pray with new passion and reminded me, *the battle is His*, and I could face the Enemy in His strength: "You're going after our kids? No, you don't!""

James went into combat-mode.

He and his wife prayed together. They had others who had been through similar circumstances, people who understood, praying for them. "When you're a parent of a prodigal, especially in the church community, you can face a lot of judgment. The truth is that every situation is unique. And it's easy to parent someone else's children."

James's son was in rehab eleven times and even went to jail several times during the seven years he was addicted to drugs and estranged from his family. He mainlined heroin and eventually became a drug dealer. With an ache in his voice, James said, "I'd read that only 15 percent of people who reach that point can turn back . . . It's only by the grace of God that our son didn't end up in prison, or dead."

As he watched his son spiral into self-destruction, James knew he was helpless on his own. "I had to cling to God in utter dependence. Going to the Word of God, looking for promises, writing them down and going back and praying them—that was my lifeline." Desperate for help, James cried out to God. "How long, Lord? How long will you let the enemy prevail over us? Do something, Lord!"

But year after year, his son drifted further away. Deliverance felt like a long shot. Should they give up on their son? Should they prepare their hearts for losing him forever? It wasn't a question of whether or not God *could* rescue their son. They had no doubt their Almighty God was able. But would they witness the Lord's deliverance and be blessed with the privilege of welcoming their prodigal home? And what were they supposed to do in the meantime?

Waiting became excruciating. Trusting the Lord to do a mighty and mysterious work of pruning a loved one's character requires us to let go of them, and it changes us, often leaving casualties and heart-penetrating scars. James now reflects on what he learned during that season of not knowing and sometimes not believing that God would rescue his son: "What's important is not to wait 'for' God, but to wait 'with' Him. If we wait with Him, He himself is the best answer to prayer. He has a way of meeting us in those places and getting us through, just because of the sweetness of His presence."

While James wrestled with his faith, his wife stood firm on her knowledge of God as a covenant God, faithful from generation to generation. She found quality care through recovery programs and would often say she *knew* the Lord would use their son in ministry someday. "The Lord enabled her to see it by faith. She saw him coming home before the fact. And then . . . do you know what our son does today? He's a youth pastor." Hallelujah!

Freed from the bondage of addiction, James's son has been clean for over six years. His goal in youth ministry is to help kids avoid making the mistakes he made by pointing them to Jesus. After a deep sigh, James said, "Sometimes we're going through things and we're just so numb. It's difficult to explain. But prayer was so huge for us. The presence of Jesus in response to prayer got us through."

Praising God, James shared a few lines from his favorite hymn by William Cowper, "God Moves in a Mysterious Way." His voice softened as he recited the lyrics: "Judge not the Lord by feeble sense, but trust Him for His grace. Behind a frowning providence, He hides a smiling face. Blind unbelief is sure to err and scan His work in vain. God is His own interpreter, and He will make it plain."

When his son was in the throes of addiction, James wrote *Prayers for Prodigals: 90 Days of Prayer for Your Child*. Almost a decade later, as James read through the prayers while recording the audio version of the book, he had to stop again and again. "My voice broke. At the time those prayers were written, they weren't answered." And now James is writing a book with his son that shares their restoration story to bring hope to other hurting families. "That's a little bit of heaven right there."

Still, as the Banks family savors the sweetness of God's presence and the heavenly joy of their son's redemption, they are still waiting for one prodigal to return. "Even today, I was crying out to the Lord for my daughter. I sincerely believe God will bring her home," he said. "I may not see her come home in this lifetime. But in the meantime, I am to persevere with passion and pray for her."

With a strong belief in the Lord's love for His wandering sheep, James created a prayer wall for prodigals on his website and leads a team at his church who prays for them. "It's an ongoing battle," said James. "What we really need when we're in the wilderness is God's presence."

When God told Moses to bring the Israelites out of Egypt, out of slavery, Moses considered his insufficiency. "Who am I that I should go to Pharaoh to bring the Israelites out of Egypt?" (Exodus 3:11). The Lord didn't give Moses a pep talk or list all of the reasons why He chose Moses. God simply said, "I will be with you" (v. 12). Moses's past service to the Lord, his credentials or pedigree, didn't matter. He had all he needed to walk through the wilderness while leading the Israelites to the Promised Land—God. And through prayer, he would communicate with God and be continually in His presence, even when he struggled with doubt, fear, frustration, and grief.

Like Moses, James learned God's presence alone would be sufficient for his impatient and weary soul. And when we feel weak, helpless, not up to the challenges ahead, we too can count on God to hear us and be with us.

We can step up, step out, and pray continually and expectantly. Our loving Father will help us rise up in victory as we fulfill His purpose for our lives and as we pray for those we love, even if they've strayed from Him . . . and even when we're the ones running from Him as we wander in the wilderness. No matter what our circumstances or how long our wait, we can depend on God to hear our prayers and rejoice as He promises, "I will be with you."

INHALE

The LORD has heard my cry for mercy;
the LORD accepts my prayer.

—PSALM 6:9

EXHALE

Listening Lord, thanks for being the God who hears us and stays with us through today and tomorrow and forever. You are our constant, dependable stronghold when we're feeling overloaded during times of trouble. Help us stand firm on the assurance of your established constancy, revealed through the ways you interact with your beloved people in the Bible.

When we're feeling stuck in the wait, please break the chains that bind us to uncertainty. When our responses are controlled by the fickleness of our feelings or our ever-changing circumstances, fill us with courageous and enduring faith. When confusion, conflict, or other folks' chaos threaten to smother our peace, please root our hope in your eternal God-breathed words of Scripture. Lord, increase our desire to seek you and commune with you during the Meantime Moments that you've ordained for us. Please help us trust you are always listening, always working for the good of those who love you, and always with us as you complete the work you've started in us . . . and others.

In Jesus's name, Amen.

- Why is it often hard to believe God is with us when tough situations drag on or our traveling path feels like a merry-go-round going nowhere fast?

- How does knowing God hears and cares about us and our loved ones help us change our perspective when we feel worn out and isolated in the wait?

• If you're praying for a prodigal or running away from God as you wander through the wilderness, please share your prayer request on the prodigal prayer wall at www.jamesbanks.org or with my blog family at www.xedixon.com.

God with Us,
you will always hear our prayers.

19

Waiting without Worrying

TODAY'S TRUTH

*When we bask in God's unchanging love,
we leave little room for worry.*

TODAY'S READING: *Luke 12:16–34*

As Hurricane Katrina caused the communities in its path to evacuate, I waited to hear from Jennifer. We'd been friends since 1989 and grew to be more like family as the years passed. I prayed for her and her sons. For hours, I called her cell repeatedly. I reached out using every form of communication available. When I couldn't reach her, worry seeped in and caused me to think the worst. Were her sons with her or had they been separated? Did they evacuate or were they stuck somewhere in the path of the natural disaster? Were they alive?

I prayed continually. I sent Jennifer's street address to all the prayer warriors who I knew would join me in fervent, specific, and confident intercession. We asked God to protect my friend and her family, to stop the waters at the curb, to prevent severe damage to their home, and to provide for them . . . wherever they were.

After the disaster destroyed much of her community, my phone rang. When I finally heard her voice, I sobbed praises to God and shared that we'd been praying for them. She recounted the many miracles of provision they'd experienced as they made their way from Louisiana to California. The Lord provided food, clothes, and safe places to stay. After hanging up, I texted the faithful prayer warriors who had comforted and encouraged me as we trusted the Lord to care for my friend. We rejoiced together. But nothing could prepare us for Jennifer's call after she returned to Louisiana.

The houses in her neighborhood had severe flood damage. One block over, the houses had two feet of water inside. Three more blocks over, the houses were under six feet of water. Her next-door neighbors had shattered windows and severely damaged rooftops. But the waters didn't even touch Jennifer's lawn. The flooding stopped at the curb. Her house had all its windows intact. Only a few shingles had been blown from her roof and onto the grass, two of which landed on top of one another. When she picked them up, she noticed a heart-shaped indentation. Feeling the Lord's loving protection, she called me to share the beautiful testimony of His goodness and thanked me for the prayers.

"I'm calling you whenever I need prayer," she said. "You have the red phone that goes straight to God."

Laughing, I assured her that the Lord hears *all* of our prayers. And since that day, we've prayed for one another. God has continually come through in mysterious and mighty ways, as we waited expectantly for His hand to move in our situations. We've praised Him together, grateful for every answer to our prayers and thankful every time we witnessed what could only be explained as God's mind-blowing grace in action. We are sure God knows our needs before we voice them, but placing each concern in His hands through prayer becomes our proclamation of that trust.

The Lord has provided, transformed hearts, and changed situations in ways we never dreamed possible. He's paved paths when there seemed to be no way around the obstacles piled high before us. If we dared create a Trust Tally—a detailed list of the awesome ways God has answered our prayers—perhaps we would more easily remember that we don't have to worry while we wait for Him to do what only He can do.

Our loving maker and sustainer assures us that He will care for us, so we don't need to fret over what we don't have or cling to what we think belongs to us. The apostle Luke introduces a story that Jesus told the crowds about a rich man who had a really successful harvest. Instead of rejoicing in God's provision and sharing his abundance generously with others, the man thought only of himself. He decided to tear down his existing barns to build bigger ones so he could store his surplus grain. Knowing he'd have "plenty of grain laid up for many years" comforted the man (v. 19). He wouldn't need to worry any longer; he'd be set for life! But he quickly learned the futility of greed and hoarding the resources God provides. He hadn't brought anything with him when he entered the world and wouldn't be able to take anything with him when he died.

After telling this story to the crowd, Jesus then turned to His disciples and said, "Therefore I tell you, do not worry about your life, what you will eat; or about your body, what you will wear. For life is more than food, and the body more than clothes" (Luke 12:22–23). Jesus proclaimed the Father would provide for all their needs and declared it pointless to fret over things they couldn't control. "For the pagan world runs after all such things, and your Father knows that you need them," He said. "But seek his kingdom, and these things will be given to you" (vv. 30–31). After offering these assuring words, Jesus said, "Do not be afraid, little flock, for your Father has been pleased to give you the kingdom" (v. 32). As the Lord affirmed their inheritance as His beloved children, He encouraged them to live with kingdom vision and a willingness to be generous with all God gave them.

God's all-knowing goodness, proven faithfulness, and consistent provision trumps anxious thoughts. As we learn to live with open hands and hearts, we can be better prepared to receive and share all the Lord has planned for us. We can stop being afraid of losing what we have or worrying about what we need. When we place our concerns in the Lord's hands, we're displaying a reliance on Him. With each prayer, we are declaring our trust in God so we can wait without worrying.

INHALE

Who of you by worrying
can add a single hour to your life?
—LUKE 12:25

EXHALE

Loving Giver of all good things, thanks for your promised provision and your established trustworthiness. Thanks for affirming we have no need to worry when we depend on your sovereign care. Please strengthen our faith and set our hearts on your kingdom.

Keep us steadfast, mighty and merciful Lord. "For great is your love, reaching to the heavens; your faithfulness reaches to the skies" (Psalm 57:10).

Please help us place every anxious thought in your hands. We accept that worry is pointless, and worse, shows our lack of faith. Help us trust your grace to be more than sufficient as you meet all our needs, even when you don't say yes to all of our requests.

When we're struggling with fear or fretting over things we can't control, please affirm you are in control and working in and through the waiting seasons of our lives. When we are tempted to worry, please give us glimpses of your grandness and reminders of every time you've come through and brought us through.

In Jesus's name, Amen.

- What Bible verses can help us to trust God when worry starts seeping into our thoughts?

- How can recording all the times the Lord has been faithful in our lives help us rely on Him, especially when circumstances cause us to feel apprehensive or fearful?

- What top ten instances would be on your Trust Tally?

- What situation do you need to place into God's hands as you prayerfully seek His care and depend on His unchanging and loving character?

Unchanging Father,
thanks for being stable and available
during uncertain times.

20

Prepared in the Pause

TODAY'S TRUTH

*God uses every pause
as an opportunity for our preparation.*

TODAY'S READING: *Matthew 25:1–13*

After completing her treatment for breast cancer, Kim Fredrickson "breathed a sigh of relief . . . for four days" before she received a new diagnosis—pulmonary fibrosis. The doctors informed her that the progressive lung disease, a rare side effect from chemotherapy and radiation, had a three- to five-year life expectancy. With the clock ticking, she entered a waiting season that seemed hopeless. As I type this chapter, I'm still praying for Kim while she waits for a lung transplant and continues to inspire others to *wait by faith* during her extended stay in the hospital.

Adjusting to life with a doctor's expiration date, Kim struggled to process her emotions until the Lord taught her how to offer herself grace—which she refers to as self-compassion in her book *The Power of Positive Self-Talk*. Kim could have easily drowned in self-pity or spent her time being angry at God, depressed over her situation, or paralyzed by hopelessness. And sometimes, she did have to work through those feelings and struggle through the grieving process. However, she chose to trust the Lord with her journey . . . no matter how long or short He decided the road ahead of her would be.

She doesn't claim to walk by faith without stumbling. Instead, she shares how she's felt God's constant "presence, assurance, and love" through the hardest moments of her wait. In all of her writings, she offers hope, encouraging readers to be kind and compassionate to themselves as readily as they would extend grace to a hurting friend. Her courageous peace inspires many as she trusts the Lord to prepare her in this *pause* He has granted her.

Kim isn't in denial and she isn't racing the clock. She admits to wishing for a "miraculous healing," but says she doesn't "feel ripped off by God." She accepts that she doesn't know the Lord's plans and affirms her trust in Him. As she allows herself to grieve in healthy and holy ways, she acknowledges her physical limitations and says it feels like her "world got suddenly smaller." She couldn't possibly have anticipated this twist in her faith-walk. But Kim has accepted every stride and every moment in stillness as an opportunity to praise the Lord and point others toward His compassionate love. On her website, she writes, "I know God has a purpose for pulmonary fibrosis in my life. He has lots of plans of how this will impact others in ways that I will never know about until Heaven."

Kim has taught me how to be a good friend to others and to myself. She demonstrates how to rest, to hurt, to grieve, and to heal while trusting God when the wait feels endless. Kim's graciousness and confident faith during her devastating pause revitalizes me when I grow weary in my waiting seasons.

Living by faith one day at a time is of greater value than recounting the number of days we've been hurting or trying to figure out how much longer we'll have to endure our trials. When we focus on our suffering, our frustrations, or the wait itself, we miss the point of all God's doing in our lives. We can even miss out on knowing Him more and experiencing His love in action.

We can walk with God in the present, being rejuvenated moment by moment by His constant and powerful presence. This world is not our home. Our hope doesn't rest in the temporal things in this life. Like Kim, our peace is rooted in the unchanging love of our Savior, Jesus Christ, not our ever-changing circumstances.

When Jesus declared His second coming in Matthew 24, He reminded the disciples that they couldn't determine the number of days until His return. Only the Father knows the day and the hour that heaven and earth will pass away. Then, in a parable, Jesus compared the kingdom of heaven to "ten virgins who took their lamps and went out to meet the bridegroom" (Matthew 25:1). The foolish ones brought lamps with no extra oil, while the wise ones came prepared with enough supplies to last through their undetermined waiting period. After waiting longer than expected, the foolish ones ran out of oil. They missed the bridegroom's arrival during their scramble for supplies. Jesus summed up the parable: "Therefore keep watch, because you do not know the day or the hour" (Matthew 25:13). Keep watch. Be ready. Remain expectant.

Through life's pauses, God prepares us to know Him more, love Him more, and serve Him according to His perfect plan. The roads we take are sometimes rocky. We often feel lost, forgotten, and worn out. But we have a promise we can cling to when we don't think we can take one more step or wait one more second: *Jesus is coming again.* "Be on guard! Be alert! You do not know when that time will come!" (Mark 13:33). God will be our strength as He carries us through each moment, even those that don't feel fair, that hurt so much we can barely stand the pain. And *when* Christ returns, He will right all wrongs, wipe away our tears, and heal all afflictions. Until then, He will continue to love us and invite us to love Him and others.

Equipped and empowered by the Holy Spirit, who dwells in us from the moment we receive Christ, we can share the gospel and spread His glory to the ends of the earth. God will carry us through when getting a grip in life feels like grasping ever-shifting shadows on a wind-kissed, sunny day. Like Kim, we can trust our faithful Father. We can rely on the power of the Holy Spirit to give us enduring hope in seemingly hopeless situations. We can praise Jesus as He prepares us for His return. And we can depend on Him to help us use every opportunity in this glorious life He's entrusted to us to share Him with others.

INHALE

May the God of hope fill you
with all joy and peace as you trust in him,
so that you may overflow with hope
by the power of the Holy Spirit.
—ROMANS 15:13

EXHALE

Holy Spirit, empower us with the surety of your constant and indwelling presence. Help us submit to your authority and live by your power as we surrender to you. Please fill us with relentless hope. Remind us that you're always guiding us and caring for us.

Faithful and compassionate Father, please prepare us for a lifetime of service, no matter how many days you've marked out for us.

Thanks for hearing us when we call on you. Thanks for assuring us of the ultimate healing you've promised us. Thanks for affirming that our weeping only lasts for a moment in light of eternity.

Please give us wisdom and courage as we stand firm on your unchanging truth and share you with love, boldness, and relentless faith.

Breathe joy and peace into our weary hearts until you call us forward in the wait. We eagerly wait for you to return, Lord Jesus.

Prepare us to thrive in the life-pauses you've ordained for our refining times of silence. Help us lean into your grace as we sing your praises.

In Jesus's name, Amen.

- When our future feels bleak, how can remembering Jesus is coming again bring us comfort, strength, and peace to face whatever comes?

- In what ways has the Lord prepared you to walk by faith during the life-pauses He's planned?

- In what area of your life could you use some self-compassion as you wait on God at the peak of your current Meantime Mountain?

Sustaining Savior,
draw us closer and help us
share you boldly.

21

Growth Takes Time

TODAY'S TRUTH

*God's planned times
of stillness are necessary
for deep-rooted spiritual growth.*

TODAY'S READING: *Mark 4:1–20*

For over a year, my husband and I felt the Lord preparing us for a move, but weren't sure where we'd end up. We imagined moving from northern to southern California. We dreamed of moving to Hawaii. But not once did either of us say, "What do you think about moving to the Midwest?" Did I mention we prefer seventy-two degrees Fahrenheit and shiver when the temperature hits sixty-eight?

When a university in Wisconsin offered Alan an interview for a job he hadn't applied for, we agreed to pray separately, to ask God to close the door if He wasn't the one leading us across the country.

Over the next few weeks, the doors to that opportunity opened so wide and the path ahead became so brightly lit that neither of us could find any reason, or excuse, to reject the offer. We didn't want to leave our sons, but were thankful they were both hardworking and independent. I didn't want to leave my doctors, but trusted God's promise to provide care wherever He led us. Neither of us wanted to leave the California weather. But as God kept on nudging us forward, we packed up and traveled across the country.

Immediately, problems with our new-to-us old home caused discouragement. Our aging dog's health declined drastically. Our new pup grew twice as big as we expected, requiring lots of exercise and training so I could walk her without further injuring my back, shoulders, and neck. Within the first month, the creek behind our house turned into a river and flooded a neighbor's basement. We experienced a mosquito uprising, the worst in over a decade. A dozen tornadoes devastated portions of our small town.

With the frustrations that came with a rushed move and my challenges with chronic pain, our optimism wavered. Our patience dwindled. Our grace toward one another stretched thin and made our last nerves more tender.

So, when a small disagreement with my husband blew up into a major argument, harsh words gushed out of my mouth. We argued over the silliest things and stomped to our silent-treatment corners. As my heart ached, I began to pray.

I had treated my husband as if he were my enemy instead of my life-partner, spiritual leader, and best friend. Before too much time passed, Alan and I asked God for forgiveness and forgave each other. We discussed the difficulties of our transition and agreed to work on our communication. But into our fifth month in Wisconsin, we were tested by a new opponent. The temperatures dropped and the winds picked up to beat the low temperatures on Mount Everest and in the Arctic. The *Arctic*.

When we got a taste of fifty degrees below zero, I feared my husband and I would slide back into unhealthy ways of dealing with conflict. Instead, by God's incredible grace, we communicated honestly, worked together, appreciated one another, and chose to demonstrate love.

My bouts with anger and sinful reactions toward my husband, however, had proved that I had more growing to do.

Behind a badge of pride, I'd had the nerve to think I was more gracious, more compassionate, and more patient—more spiritually mature—than the one who'd offended me. I was wrong . . . so wrong. I decided to return to a prayer I used to say almost daily.

Lord, please change me and make me more like you.

It's tempting to desire immediate transformation in a world that seems bent toward instant gratification. But spiritual growth is a lifelong process that takes time. God requires and uses every precious second of the wait to make His life-changes stick. It's through our trust-induced surrender to the Lord's constant pruning that He nurtures growth.

Jesus painted a beautiful and humbling image of what His disciples could expect in their ongoing spiritual development. In the parable of the sower, a farmer intentionally "went out to sow his seed" (Mark 4:3). Some fell along the path and didn't even have a chance to sink in before the birds enjoyed a tasty snack. A few seeds landed on rocky places covered with just enough soil for the sprouts to grow, but their shallow roots withered when the heat rose. Other seeds took root and grew but were too weak to thrive among surrounding thorns. But the farmer also managed to plant some of the seeds in good soil, rich and ready soil that produced a healthy crop, "some multiplying thirty, some sixty, some a hundred times" (v. 8).

Before the disciples could get too excited about a future in gardening, Jesus explained that the farmer in His story sowed the Word of God (vv. 13–14). Some folks hear but don't *receive* God's truth; belief is superficial at best. Some hearts hear and receive the word with joy-filled immediacy but, since their commitment is shallow, "they quickly fall away" when trouble comes (v. 17). For others, the "worries of this life, the deceitfulness of wealth and the desires for *other things* come in and choke the word, making it unfruitful" (vv. 18–19, emphasis mine). But there are those who endure the storms in life, by the power of the Holy

Spirit and who welcome the long-term sifting that enriches their heart-soil. These folks seek the Lord *above other things*, hear the Word, and *accept it* as unfailing and dependable, unchanging and life-transforming truth. They can enjoy a fruitful life, cultivated through the daily nurturing and deep rooting of their Spirit-empowered faith in the God-breathed words of Scripture (v. 20).

It was eye-opening to realize my heart went through every stage of the farmer's garden in the parable. Sometimes, I knew what Scripture said but rejected God's commands. Sometimes my hardened heart wanted to accept and obey God's truth, but couldn't keep my sinfulness from rearing its ugly head. When my thorny attitude got the best of me, I allowed fear and worry to guide my reactions. And by God's amazing grace, there were also times when I wisely spent time with the Lord and invited Him to nourish and sift the soil of my heart with His truth. During those glorious moments, I surrendered to Him out of love-laced faith. When I remained connected to God, I was more likely to invite Him to prune my fleshly wants so I could respond to conflict in ways that allowed me to reflect His character.

Our growth requires pruning and even death. Death of relationships. Death of grudges. Death of hopes, obligations, dreams, and expectations. Death of selfishness. Death of sin. Each loss and each triumph can deepen our relationship with Jesus and strengthen our testimony . . . or not.

We can focus on our outward appearance and allow spiritual pride to tempt us to become complacent. We can try to hold it together, primping and preening so we look super-spiritual. But those closest to us often get to see the rawness of our real selves, our works-in-progress selves. Our spiritual growth requires a lifetime commitment to following God, an ongoing dependency on Him . . . one day and sometimes one breath at a time.

God has given us a gift that cannot be returned or replenished—time. Since we can't control this commodity, it would be wise to submit to the one who can. So, without a moment to waste, we can ask the Time Keeper to help us trust His direction, empower us to persevere, and show us the next step in this great faith adventure.

INHALE

Be joyful in hope,
patient in affliction,
faithful in prayer.
—ROMANS 12:12

EXHALE

You are so good, so faithful, and so thorough in the ways you deal with us, mighty God.

Thanks for seeing the potential you've placed in us, the potential we haven't even begun to realize. Please keep us focused on you and dependent on you during the pruning of our character and the strengthening of our faith.

Please help us compare ourselves to you, the only one who is holy and righteous, instead of others who are just as imperfect as we are. When we get comfortable with complacency, we invite you to shake things up so you can deepen our faith.

Help us persist with Spirit-empowered confidence as you grow us and others, according to your perfect plan and pace.

In Jesus's name, Amen.

- How does it help you to know God remains patient as He nurtures your spiritual growth?

- How do you deal with those moments when you slip back into the struggle against old sins that remind you how much more you have to grow to be Christlike?

- What sinful attitude or action do you need God to prune out of your life today?

Mighty Maker of time itself,
please make us more like you.

22

Soul-Strengthening Silence

TODAY'S TRUTH

God is still sovereign in the silence.

TODAY'S READING: *Psalm 77*

I studied my mom as she generously offered a listening ear, wise counsel, and genuine kindness to her fellow fighters at the cancer care center. No matter how worn out she felt after a long day of appointments, she made herself available to spread spirit-refreshing faith. She leaned forward when she listened to weary patients sharing their concerns. Her eyes revealed sincere concern. Her smile reflected compassion and peace with her Hope-Giver. She whispered comforting words resounding with unquestionable faith. Her voice never wavered with worry. Her hands never trembled with fear or doubt. But her soul-strengthening silence inspired me most.

Mom strolled a few feet ahead of me on the second-floor walking path. Her stride slowed on the harder days. Still, she smiled at passers-by and occasionally stopped for a quick chat. Some folks went out of their way to connect with her. Maybe they longed for a friendly face. Maybe they enjoyed her uplifting messages. Maybe they just wanted to be close to her in hopes of feeding off the power of faith she exuded.

I followed her up to the rooftop garden and sat in a chair next to her, admiring her tenacity. The warm knit hat that hid her balding head framed her lovely face. She sighed as she stared out at the horizon.

"Are you okay, Mom?"

She inhaled, closing her eyes, then exhaled with her lips melting into a grin. "I'm at peace."

"You look tired," I said.

She nodded. "I am."

As I considered my own healing journey and my daily battle with chronic pain, I thanked God for giving me the strength I needed to serve as my mom's live-in caregiver despite my weakness. "I'm tired, too, Mom."

She wrung her wrinkling hands then placed them on her lap. "God's in control," she said. "I feel Him with me." Her eyes glistened as she met my gaze. "He's never let us down before." She reminisced on how the Lord had worked in and through our lives, how He had carried us through each day after her diagnosis. Then, with a sigh and a smile, she turned toward the evening sky and spoke her watchword with assurance. "May His will be done . . . not mine."

We sat quietly, side by side, until the soft breeze turned into a cool nip and the sun set.

Gazing over the skyline and the hills in the distance, I enjoyed the splendor of God as He painted the skies with shades of orange and grey. I basked in the peace of His presence. I had grown weary because I had been neglecting my much-needed moments with God. When had I started trying to walk in my own strength? When had I stopped depending on the Lord to refresh my spirit day-to-day? When had I settled for running on empty instead of relying on His grace one breath at a time? "I cried out to God for help; I cried out to God to hear me. When I was in distress, I sought the Lord; at night I stretched out untiring hands, and I would not be comforted" (Psalm 77:1–2).

My mom's battle with cancer tested my faith. As I focused on my current circumstances and fretted over my countless limitations, doubt trickled into my prayers. My heart cries echoed those of the psalmist who sang, "I remembered you, God, and I groaned; I meditated, and my spirit grew faint" (v. 3).

Shortly after that rooftop chat, though, my love for Jesus and my mom changed my desires and my prayers from self-centered to Christ-centered. I stopped pushing God for answers and concerning myself with the duration of the wait. I stopped begging the Lord to strengthen my mom so she could keep fighting. I stopped pleading for relief and the steadfastness necessary to endure the long road ahead. Instead, like my mom, I submitted and asked Him to align my will to His.

God anchored my hope in His promises, His sovereignty, and His endless love for us. Even His silence in the wait strengthened my soul as I leaned on the guarantee of His never-changing character. I could depend on Jesus because He is and always will be *the* way and *the* truth and *the* life. I could be sure that God's way is perfect because He is perfect.

As I served my mom during the wait, I still expected and prayed for a miracle of His healing grace. The Lord was able. I believed with all of my heart He would grant us a glorious testimony of His healing grace. Instead, He prepared me for one of the hardest goodbyes I would ever face. With the confidence of the psalmists' songs, my mother declared her binding belief in the Lord's goodness. Walking with dependence on His moment-by-moment mercy, she said goodbye to each of our family members . . . for now.

Following her legacy, my growing surety in God's infallible transcendence and timeliness became my safeguard against doubt as I grieved and moved forward. Years later, I still blink back grateful tears as I remember my heart-shifting moment on that Seattle rooftop.

God's past and promised faithfulness echo through His soul-strengthening silence. When the Meantime Mountains block our view of hope in the horizon, we can "remember the deeds of the LORD," recollecting His "miracles of long ago" (v. 11). We can ponder all His works, all His mighty deeds. We can praise Him for His holiness and affirm His power over all creation.

Walking by faith requires living in the present moment and being sure of God's constant presence to empower perseverance. We can count on Christ's proven faithfulness, His unchanging character, and His promise to return. As we rest, secure in His unconditional love and unrelenting grace, our spirits can be revitalized so we can rise up in victorious praise at just the right time . . . His time. God uses every soul-strengthening moment of silence to refine our faith. He is as trustworthy as His power is limitless, especially when the wait feels endless.

INHALE

You are the God who performs miracles;
you display your power among the peoples.
—PSALM 77:14

EXHALE

Good Father, thanks for affirming your majesty and never-ending mercy. Thanks for reminding us that you are not surprised by the circumstances that blindside us. You prepare us, watch over us, and meet our deepest needs with such lovingkindness.

When the Meantime Mountains block our view of your hope-filled horizon, please remind us that you are always good, always working, always with us, and always in control.

When worry or fear tempt us to doubt your abounding power, please affirm your infinite reach and ongoing faithfulness. Strengthen our resolve with the comfort of your constant presence.

Please, Lord, help us trust your silence as much as we trust your yes, your no, your maybe, and your not yet.

Help us come to you with bold obedience and praise you with unbridled passion as we exalt your name, Lord.

Your plan is perfect. Your pace is perfect. You are perfect, Lord.

As we walk with you and wait on you, help us recognize our weaknesses as opportunities to experience your power. Make us strong in you as we rely on you, the One who shapes the clouds, controls the winds, and directs the waters.

There is no one like you, Lord Almighty. May your name be glorified and your power magnified as we rejoice in your endless love and enduring hope.

In Jesus's name, Amen.

- Why does it feel harder to be still when God seems to be silent?

- How has the Lord proven His faithfulness, His sovereignty, and His goodness in your life?

- In what current situation are you waiting to hear from God?

- What attribute of God can help you trust His plan and pace in that situation?

Ever-present God,
you made it all, own it all,
and work in and through it all.

23
Working in the Wait

TODAY'S TRUTH

Working with God
is worshipping God in the wait.

TODAY'S READING: *Matthew 25:14–30*

Shortly after her thirtieth birthday, Lynn started experiencing severe headaches, facial swelling, and vision problems. She went to multiple doctors and left each one without a diagnosis or relief from her increasing pain. Waiting, without answers, Lynn battled frustration and fear. Would she have to deal with these worsening symptoms all of her life?

Finally, she received a diagnosis: brain tumor. Relief flowed over her as she considered the possibility of a cure, until a whole new set of fears welled up inside of her. Would she be blind or paralyzed after the surgery? Would the procedure even work? As she faced the what-ifs, Lynn relied on her belief that God would bring her through whatever came her way. She knew her life would be different. She knew she'd have to trust God as she waited for Him to work out her health issues. But she didn't know if she'd ever realize her hope-filled dream of becoming a wife and mother.

Lynn didn't allow health complications to stop her from serving the Lord joyfully or consistently, though. With Spirit-empowered strength and courage, and her doctor's approval, she left for Mexico with a missionary group from our church two days after her diagnosis. She returned, taught a weeklong vacation Bible school, and then had surgery. A few months later, she went right on back to work as a teacher of children with special needs.

Despite suffering from side effects, Lynn moved on and continued trusting the Lord. She waited for God to show her the next step toward her still-unfulfilled dreams of being a wife and mom. As she climbed her Meantime Mountains and hiked through rocky-pathed valleys of suffering, Lynn used her gift of loving well to serve as a babysitter for most of the children in our church family. She cared for the elderly, worked countless hours in the church, and even served as my caregiver after one of my more complicated surgeries. If someone needed help, Lynn was first in line to offer her assistance. She inspired others to approach service as an opportunity to worship the Lord.

As her friend, I understood the longings of her heart, and I prayed for her. I realized one of her most selfless acts of service involved her leadership as a wedding coordinator at our church. When she helped couples organize the details of their big day, surrounded by love stories, fragrant flowers, and fancy wedding cakes, Lynn longed for the day God would allow her to have her own husband and start her own family. Though she insisted God's plan and pace were always perfect, she struggled with discouragement during the wait.

The days felt longer as she slipped from her early thirties into her late thirties. Friends set her up on dates and gave advice, often unsolicited, on how to land a man. When several folks told Lynn she needed to set aside her standards and head out to the local bars if she wanted to find her husband, she refused. But she began to lose hope.

Before Lynn could release her dream, she decided to give dating one more shot. If God could be trusted with her brain tumor and the painful side effects she still endures daily since

her surgery, He could certainly be trusted with her heart-desire
of becoming a wife and mother. She determined to keep her
commitment to God as her first priority and decided to try an
online Christian dating service. Through it, she met a man who
had been praying for a godly spouse. Though he lived only a
few miles away and they shared the same circle of friends, they
had not met. They started dating and almost immediately began
serving the Lord together. They got married a year later and
three years later gave birth to a beautiful son, . . . in God's perfect time. Now, they use their unique God-given gifts to faithfully serve the Lord as a family . . . Hallelujah!

Lynn and her husband know they're saved by grace, not by
works of service (Ephesians 2:8–10). As a married couple, they've
faced their fair share of trials. But when they consider all God's
done for them, they delight in using their talents wisely, generously, continually, and for God's glory, wherever the Lord leads
them.

Jesus shared a parable about a man "going on a journey, who
called his servants and entrusted to them his property" (Matthew 25:14 ESV). He expected them to be wise stewards of all
he'd given them. "To one he gave five talents, to another two,
to another one, to each according to his ability. Then he went
away" (v. 15 ESV). The first two servants invested what their master had given them and experienced a return. "But he who had
received the one talent went and dug in the ground and hid his
master's money" (v. 18). When the master returned and "settled
accounts with them," he rewarded the two servants who used
their talents and rebuked the one who cowered in fear, refusing
to invest his talents.

In this parable, Jesus used a measure of weight—talents—
to show the value of what the master had given his servants.
With the modern meaning of "talents," we can use this mes-
sage to recognize how the need for being a faithful steward can
apply to all God has given us, from material resources to our

natural abilities. God gives us ample opportunities to invest all He's entrusted to us—not just finances but also skills, abilities, experiences, and even time—for the benefit of others and for His glory.

Worshipping the Lord makes our working in the wait-time more than productive. Through our service, God nurtures the roots of our faith and prepares us for the plan He has designed for us, a plan that impacts others. As members of the interdependent church, our time and abilities are valuable and necessary for our good and the good of others. Our days are connected to the day-to-day lives of those we know and those God hasn't yet brought into our lives. When we invest in others, through acts of service or intercessory prayer, waiting becomes a time of preparation and heart-transforming praise.

INHALE

Now to him who is able to do immeasurably
more than all we ask or imagine,
according to his power that is at work within us,
to him be glory in the church and
in Christ Jesus throughout all generations,
for ever and ever! Amen.
—EPHESIANS 3:20–21

EXHALE

Generous Father, thanks for creating us and blessing us with talents, skills, abilities, and experiences to use as we serve you and your people. Help us wait on your direction, follow your leading, and remain focused on serving you and worshipping you with gladness.

Affirm you are always at work in us, even when we feel like we're standing still in the wait. Please fill us with the courage and confidence we need to make the most of every opportunity you give us to develop and share the gifts you've entrusted to us.

Help us to be good stewards of the resources you've provided, instead of grumbling about what we don't have or what you're not doing.

Forgive us when we are selfish and lazy and resist the work you have planned for us to do. Please help us serve you with selflessness, faithfulness, and thankfulness, as we trust your plan to unfold in your perfect timing.

Thank you, Lord, for reminding us that you are trustworthy and loving as we delight in you and wait expectantly for you to work all things out for the good of all those who love you.

In Jesus's name, Amen.

- How can worshipping God by serving others help adjust our perspective and increase our patience?

- How has the Lord used the time you've worked in the wait to prepare you to receive an answer to prayer?

- How is the Lord nudging you to use the gifts He's entrusted to you?

Great Provider,
please give us opportunities
to worship you by serving you.

24

Lacking Nothing

TODAY'S TRUTH

*God's way includes well-planned provision
through the wait.*

TODAY'S READING: *Psalm 23*

Crystal and Bob Bowman looked forward to becoming grand-parents and were pleased when their oldest son got married and announced their first baby.

Some time later, though, Crystal struggled to find the right response when her youngest son shared that he and his wife, Meghann, wanted a baby but it just wasn't happening. "We're doing everything we can," he said.

Crystal and Bob assured the young couple that they were not alone, and promised to pray for them through this painful journey. But none of the family members expected how dark and lonely the journey would be or how this trek through the wait would impact all of their lives. For years, they prayed for Meghann to conceive. Time kept on passing. Life moved on all around them.

"It was hard," says Crystal. "In the meantime, my other children were having babies. I would talk to Meghann, to let her know that I understood it was painful for them. I was proud of them for rejoicing with others, even when they were having a hard time. I just kept praying God would fill their home with children according to His plan."

Once, Bob took their youngest son on a vacation for a one-day climb on Mount Fuji. When they got to the top of the mountain, the men looked over God's creation. Bob said, "Someday, maybe you can do this with your son." When his grown child broke down and sobbed, Bob embraced him and joined in his grief. He offered no words of advice, no encouragement, no Bible verses. He just put his arm around his son and wept with him until they went down the mountain together.

After their experience, Crystal's son shared how deeply his father's actions impacted him. "That's exactly what I needed," he said. "I needed someone to share my grief. I didn't need advice, a pep talk, or medical knowledge. I just needed someone to feel my pain with me."

Even though the doctors had told this young couple they would most likely never have children naturally, they kept trying. They pursued acupuncture, natural medicine, and did lots of research. They finally decided to try an IVF procedure and were devastated when it resulted in an early miscarriage. They waited and waited, tried and tried, until they "couldn't do it anymore." Weary and weak, they decided to do the most courageous and most difficult thing they could during the darkest time of their marriage . . . completely surrender to God. They chose to stop fighting against infertility.

Five years after they began their sorrow-filled sojourn, they were able to flourish in the peace of God's loving presence. They were finally able to see that they had lacked nothing all along the way . . . even when they faced hard days. One Sunday, they invited Crystal and her husband to join them for church and brunch. After the waitress placed their food in front of them, Crystal's daughter-in-law smiled. "I have a picture I want to show you," she said. She pulled out an envelope and handed her in-laws a sonogram photo.

There was no question about how to respond this time. With people seated at tables all around them, they wept for joy.

The family thanked God for their beautiful blessing, while realizing that not all stories of infertility end with a miraculous pregnancy. Some couples choose adoption. A rare few adopt, and then give birth to a biological child. But not all couples praying to be parents end up with a child in the home. During the pregnancy and the birth of her beautiful baby, Meghann's heart still ached—for those still enduring the wait as they trusted God through the valley of infertility.

During a conversation with her mother-in-law, Meghann shared that God was prompting her to write a book so other women would not have to suffer alone. "When you're struggling with infertility, it seems like everyone around you is pregnant," she said. "You get baby shower invitations and want to be happy for people. But all you see are pregnant women. It's such a dark and lonely time."

And everyone's infertility story is different. Meghann now has two healthy babies. But her results aren't common, so she wanted many women to share their stories—women of various ages, different ethnicities, from all walks of life, with different infertility stories. So Crystal came alongside her daughter-in-law to write *Mothers in Waiting: Healing and Hope for Those with Empty Arms*. With this book, women who are experiencing infertility will have 30 women to walk beside them. Each chapter ends with hope, pointing readers to God.

Crystal and Meghann asked contributors to share their "raw and honest testimonies." Some share stories about IVF failures and successes, about surgeries and adoption. One person had over a dozen miscarriages. Some women went to counseling. Some didn't. Some have children in their home now. Some don't. But somehow, all have surrendered to God and are experiencing His peace.

"The journey is hard, no matter what the outcome," says

Crystal. Depending on God's sovereignty means believing His *no* is as necessary to His greater plan as His *yes*.

Our Good Shepherd provides for all our needs and knows when it's best to make us "lie down in green pastures" or lead us "beside quiet waters" during the wait (Psalm 23:2). He knows when the journey is too much for us to handle. He knows when we need our spirits refreshed and our strength replenished for the long roads ahead. He doesn't stop working when we're resting, though. We can trust God to lead us because He is the only one who can know what lies ahead, what needs will come, and what we're truly ready to receive.

Our loving Father doesn't always take us out of difficult situations, but He will not leave us without protection, provisions, and the comfort of knowing He's right there with us. We don't have to cower before the enemies who doubt our faith or God's ability, even when our greatest adversary mocks us from our very own mirrors. No matter what our situation, God's goodness and love cannot be thwarted. The Lord uses every moment in the valley of waiting for a purpose much grander than our instant gratification or immediate relief. Even when we succumb to our weaknesses and place our wants above God, His love pursues us. Faith empowers us to wait with expectation in *this* moment.

As we remain focused on God *in the present*, we can walk and wait without fretting over what we don't have, what we don't see, and what we don't understand. Our compassionate and loving Father knows exactly what we need. Our Good Shepherd maintains control and authority, even in the wait. When we place our hope in the Lord, we will want for nothing because He'll become our everything.

INHALE

The LORD is my shepherd, I lack nothing.
—PSALM 23:1

EXHALE

All-Sufficient Savior, we love you and worship you. Thanks for affirming you always have been and always will be Lord of Lords and King of Kings, Protector and Planner, and loving Father to all you have made.

Help us know you intimately, as we stand firm on the integrity of your character. Give us assurance in your abilities and characteristics. Comfort us with your ongoing presence.

We come before you with grateful praise, fully dependent on your enduring love and faithfulness.

Please refresh our spirits as we persevere, no matter where you lead us. Help us honor you as we walk and wait in steadfast faith one day, one moment, one breath at a time.

In Jesus's name, Amen.

- How has the Lord used others to encourage you during times of waiting?

- What verses do you go to for support when the wait feels too long or too hard?

- As you reflect on past experiences in the wait, how did God show you He was still in control, still working, still providing, and still comforting you?

- Who can you pray for and encourage this week by sharing a verse or a few verses that God has used to help you persevere through the wait?

Good Shepherd,
thanks for your faithful provision
throughout the wait.

25

Ready or Not

TODAY'S TRUTH

God is always prepared,
whether we feel ready or not.

TODAY'S READING: *Joshua 1—4*

Throughout the years of serving as youth leaders, my husband and I had the privilege of investing in the lives of some inspiring teenagers. One of our students, Jared, walked to our weekly youth group meetings and to church on Sunday. Even though his parents didn't attend services, he remained dedicated to seeking the Lord and was baptized before his senior year in high school.

During spring break, we took the seniors in the youth group to a country obstacle course to help them learn about the need for trusting God and the power of being connected within a community of believers. As the students slipped on the harnesses and prepared to walk the tightrope, I reminded them that God's Word could keep our feet on the narrow road of righteousness that often feels like a rope tethered over the Grand Canyon. When they readied themselves to climb an eight-foot wall, I shared how important it was to surround ourselves with fellow believers to encourage us, pray for us, and give us a helping hand when we grow weary of climbing the Meantime Mountains in life. The group laughed together and cheered each other on as they navigated the various obstacles. We assured them that, ready or not, they would need God and each other as they headed out into the world.

Shortly after our obstacle course training session and right before graduation, Jared called to ask for counsel and prayer. "I've got a huge decision to make," he said. "What if I make the wrong choice?"

Jared had spent time in prayer and wanted to be sure he was following God and not his own desires. He'd dreamed of joining the military since middle school. But his family had other plans for his future, plans that included a college close to home. Though he knew what he wanted to do after graduation, Jared couldn't seem to shake his fear of failure or disappointing his family. If accepted into the program he had his mind set on, he would be shipped to boot camp almost immediately after graduation and would most likely serve overseas. "I'll be far from home, with no support," he said. "What if I'm not ready?"

I prayed silently before assuring him that the Lord had already paved the way for us. Though He's given us free will to choose whether or not to follow Him, our sovereign God already knows the way we'll decide to go. "We won't surprise the Lord with our decisions, good or bad," I said. "Whether we *feel* ready or not, we can move forward with confidence and know God will help us when we seek Him. We can be at peace, simply because God *will* be with us . . . no matter how long or lonely the road ahead may seem."

Jared sighed. "I'm nervous about how long I'll be away from my family."

"And I'm excited to see the amazing things God has in store for you, no matter what you decide."

After praying for this courageous young man of faith, I rejoiced in how much the Lord had done in his life. I kept him in prayer when he shipped out and enjoyed a successful military career. During some of the longer, lonelier stretches between visits home during leave, Jared couldn't seem to feel God's presence.

He called us a few times. Each time, we prayed with him. We assured him that our all-knowing and always faithful God would remain true to His Word in the wait and when He led His children into new territory.

Following God isn't always easy, especially when we're not sure about what lies down the road and around the corner. We read in the Old Testament that when Joshua stepped into his leadership position after the death of Moses, the Lord assured him that He had great plans for the Israelites (Joshua 1). He promised His constant presence and the security and hope available to those who rested in the center of His will. The Lord offered these wise words of encouragement sealed with a promise: "Have I not commanded you? Be strong and courageous. Do not be afraid; do not be discouraged, *for* the LORD your God will be with you wherever you go" (v. 9, emphasis mine). God affirms we can be brave because of His ongoing presence.

Joshua responded in bold obedience, refusing to rush the Lord's timing. When they prepared to cross the Jordan River and take possession of the land, he told the people to get ready. "Consecrate yourselves, for tomorrow the LORD will do amazing things among you" (Joshua 3:5). Eagerly waiting for God to prove His faithfulness, this leader encouraged the Israelites as they broke camp. He prepared them to follow the priests toward the river bank at flood stage. "As soon as the priests who carried the ark reached the Jordan and their feet touched the water's edge, the water from upstream stopped flowing. It piled up in a heap a great distance away . . . so the people crossed over opposite Jericho" (vv. 15–16).

The Lord stopped the waters and cleared the way for His obedient people to follow His command. The priests stood on dry ground in the middle of the once flooding river, "while all Israel passed by until the whole nation had completed the crossing *on dry ground*" (v. 17, emphasis mine). The Almighty completely cut off the flow of the flooding waters and dried out the muddied river bottom, demonstrating His awesome power and His ongoing presence with His people. The Israelites didn't know if the wall of water would cave in and drown them, yet they walked by faith across the miraculously dried path that God had placed before them. They trusted Him until they could look back and rejoice over what He'd done.

Following God's command, Joshua took twelve stones that had been gathered from the place where the priests stood in the middle of the Jordan (Joshua 4). When he stepped into his role as leader, Joshua inspired others toward great faith and led with courage. The same God who made a way for His people to cross the Red Sea is the same God who stopped the flooding waters of the Jordan River. The same God promises He will remain with His people . . . then and now. He is the same God who infused our young friend Jared with persevering boldness of faith as he served his country, started a family, and went on to become a strong spiritual leader within his sphere of influence.

God empowers us to wait and move forward with confidence. No matter what obstacles lie ahead of us or how long and treacherous our journey feels, our loving Lord remains with us. Whether we feel ready or not, God will be our strength and provide all we need for our faith-walk.

INHALE

Sustain me, my God,
according to your promise, and I will live;
do not let my hopes be dashed.
—PSALM 119:116

EXHALE

Lord God our King, thanks for being with us as you lead us down the paths you've marked out for us. Thanks for preparing us for every obstacle we'll face and providing for our every need.

Your unfathomable greatness secures our hope in your ability to do above and beyond all we can even begin to imagine.

As we meditate on your awesome works, we celebrate your abundant goodness and rejoice in your righteousness.

You are faithful, mighty, and merciful. Thanks for watching over us, for being near to us, for saving us, Lord God Almighty.

When we face big decisions and uncertain times, please give us wisdom and discernment. Please help us remember you hear us and are always working in and through us.

We build our trust on the solid foundation of your truth and the knowledge of who you are and what you've done. Help us stride with confidence as we follow you, prepared with enduring hope that your reach extends beyond our personal space. Whether we feel ready or not, help us know you're always ready and always able.

In Jesus's name, Amen.

- Describe a time when you felt unprepared to move forward, but chose to follow God's leading and trust His faithfulness.

- What has God done to help you feel strong and courageous when you didn't feel ready to take a big step?

- What attributes of God can help you trust Him when you can't seem to feel His presence?

All-Knowing Father,
nothing we do today
will surprise you at all.

26

Just Wait and See!

TODAY'S TRUTH

God's schedule includes miracles
we do not want to miss.

TODAY'S READING: *John 11:1–44*

Craig's anger simmered. How could a doctor inform his wife she only had three months to live when she sat in a room alone? Why didn't he wait for her family to arrive? After discovering his wife had undiagnosed cancer for fifteen years and now could expect only ninety days left with them, Craig couldn't wait to give the doctor an earful.

But when he realized the limited amount of time he had with his wife, when he considered the short months they would share with their children, when he saw her beautiful face . . . he decided not to waste his energy on something he couldn't change. God would bring them through this challenging time. He'd been faithful before. He'd be faithful again. Wouldn't He?

Craig wanted to—*needed* to—savor every moment with his family. Serving as Sandi's caregiver while raising their sons proved to be more than a full-time commitment. He was hurt but not surprised when he lost the job to which he had devoted twenty-three years of service. Surely God would take care of them as he cared for his family. So he walked by faith, waited by faith, and hated to admit that he sometimes worried when he lacked faith as they approached the three-month mark. He pleaded with God for mercy, longing for a miraculous healing. He prayed, afraid to hope but more afraid to be a widower. Nine months after Sandi's diagnosis, Craig lost his beloved wife. He thanked the Lord for the extra six months He'd given them, clueless to the wearisome waiting he would still face as he entered his "restart season."

Mountains of medical bills and piles of responsibilities and commitments with kids weighed heavy on this newly widowed father. When his job loss led to overwhelming financial trouble, homelessness, and emotional turmoil, despair overcame Craig. "Lord, how can I tell my kids we have no place to live, that I have no money for gas, for food, for anything? Why aren't you coming to my rescue?" As he cried out in frustration, Craig recognized his fear-laced requests were filled with doubt.

With no hope in sight, no strength to hang on, no faith to anchor him, this worn out single dad called out to his Father with a surrendered heart: "Lord, I have nothing left to believe with. I may not have 100 percent to offer, but I'll give you 100 percent of what I have."

As he surrendered and clung to the promises of God's sovereign goodness and proven faithfulness, Craig witnessed everyday miracles. Although he didn't experience the instant rescue he wanted, Craig thanked the Lord for using His people to meet his family's needs . . . one day . . . one moment . . . and often one meal at a time. Before he could fret over what he didn't have enough of, folks showed up with gas cards, groceries, and clothes for his growing boys. One man who had been praying for Craig offered the family an affordable home to rent. He'd had no idea they had been homeless and depending on others for temporary places to stay.

Craig admits that if he would have been rescued immediately, he would have missed out on the outpour of faith-solidifying examples of God's unconditional and life-transforming love.

Though the journey proved tough and overwhelming at times, he appreciated God's ever-flowing grace in the meantime. Craig encountered the love of His Father more and more intimately with every opportunity he'd been given to become reliant on His constant presence and moment-by-moment provision. "Sometimes the process we have to go through is for someone else more than for ourselves," he says.

As Craig raises his own young men, he now hosts The RZNG-MEN radio show, "where men have *RealTalk* about *RealLife*." He interviews guests with powerful testimonies of God's faithfulness and inspires others to live with bold faith and confident surrender to Christ. "We all have to get to the place with God," Craig says, "where we're good with His plan in its entirety." He affirms that God is wonderfully good, even when life is terribly hard.

Knowing the value of patient and persevering faith, Jesus taught His disciples to trust His plan as well as His pace. When Lazarus lay sick in his bed in Bethany, his sisters sent word to Jesus. The Lord responded, "This sickness will not end in death. No, it is for God's glory so that God's Son may be glorified through it" (John 11:4).

Scripture affirms Jesus loved Lazarus and his sisters, yet when He heard that Lazarus was sick, Jesus stayed put two more days. Why would He do that? Why wouldn't He rush to comfort them with His physical presence? Why wouldn't He immediately heal His friend when He had proven He had the power to do so by simply speaking? Why? Because Jesus loved them . . . *so* . . . because of his love for them . . . He comforted them with a promise. Jesus delayed their return to Judea *because* He loved Lazarus and his sisters, as well as the disciples. Though reasons abounded for them to steer clear of the area, that's not why He waited; the Lord had a greater purpose for postponing their trip—He planned to resurrect Lazarus. "So then he told them plainly, 'Lazarus is dead, and for your sake I am glad I was not there, *so that* you may believe" (v. 14–15, emphasis mine).

When they arrived, Lazarus had been in the tomb for four days. Witnesses gathered around the grieving sisters, Mary and Martha, who greeted the Lord with broken hearts. When Jesus told them to open the tomb, Martha worried about the odor of the dead body. She didn't even consider the possibility of Jesus blessing them with a wonder, the glory of God shining through a miracle of resurrection, right before their eyes. "Then Jesus said, 'Did I not tell you that if you believe, you will see the glory of God?'" (v. 40). In an awesome act of love, Jesus demonstrated the magnitude of His power "for the benefit" of those watching, of those who rolled away the stone from the front of the tomb, of those who would hear about what Jesus did in Bethany . . . that we "may believe" the Father sent Him (vv. 41–42). When He called Lazarus to rise from the dead, Jesus affirmed His divinity and many put their faith in Him on that day.

Each minute of the wait-time, planned with precision by the Maker of Time, welcomed the disciples—and all who read the Scriptures—to witness His mercy and might in action.

When trials are perilous and the wait feels endless, it's tempting to beg for an immediate rescue or instant relief. Fear-laced prayer requests poured out in desperation keep us bound in doubt. As we rely on God, though, He pumps up our faith-muscles and musters up the courage and strength we need to surrender to His every move. The Lord has every intention of remaining true to His Word, being with us constantly, loving us unconditionally, and providing for us at the right time. God makes sure His wondrous works are always worth the wait. Just wait and see!

INHALE

Then Jesus said,
"Did I not tell you that if you believe,
you will see the glory of God?"
—JOHN 11:40

EXHALE

Marvelous Time Keeper, thanks for affirming you are all-powerful, all-knowing, all-good, and always in control. You are always with us and always working all things out for the good of those who love you. Thanks for reminding us that others are watching as you are working in and through our lives. May your name be glorified, mighty Jesus!

Even when our circumstances feel utterly impossible, you've already made a way for us to walk in brave faith. You equip us to overcome, even when the odds are stacked against us.

Thanks for using others to minister to our needs, as you use us to serve others for the glory of your name. We can rely on you to know what we need and when we need it, Lord.

When the wait drags on and drains our patience, please give us peace secured in the surety of your presence and your unchanging character. Help us remember your generosity never falls short, your lovingkindness never fails us, and your grace never leaves us with insufficiencies.

In Jesus's name, Amen.

- In what situation have you offered or are you currently offering fear-laced prayer requests?

- How has God provided for you in seemingly impossible circumstances?

- In what area of your life have you struggled to believe God?

- What attributes of God help you with your unbelief?

Jesus, Savior, open our eyes
to see you are working in the wait.

27

Something to Celebrate

TODAY'S TRUTH

*God's work in the wait
is worth celebrating.*

TODAY'S READING: *Luke 15:11–32*

Over fifteen years ago, I met a woman whom I disliked and who just about loathed me. By God's incredible grace, we worked through the miscommunication that had divided us, and Cendy is now one of my closest friends.

When doctors diagnosed one of her children with juvenile diabetes, we committed to praying for all of our sons boldly. Over the years, we've interceded for our children, watching and waiting for God to move in and through their lives. Sometimes our prayers have been answered quickly and according to our hopes. Sometimes our prayers seemed to slam against the ceiling, bounce back, and smack us in our faces.

It didn't take long to come to an agreement: Parenting is one of the toughest and most rewarding lifelong acts of service to the Lord. Why, oh why, was it easier to trust Jesus when our kids were under the shelter of our overprotective wings? Those children have all professed their faith in Christ and have grown into young men with kind hearts, great work ethics, and compassion for others. They spend more time away from us, more time influenced by those who don't love the Lord. We knew we couldn't control what our children did or what happened to them. We knew God would hear us and answer us when we prayed. Still, in our weak moments, we struggled with anxious thoughts about our sons' futures. We fretted over how they'd handle the circumstances when they made poor choices . . . or at least choices that we didn't agree were the best.

A bit of introspective motive-searching revealed that some of our prayers were pleas to have our sons develop into the men we wanted them to be, instead of the men God created them to be. We preferred they avoid suffering, even though we knew God often used hardships to create beautiful testimonies of His grace. We preferred they make the decisions we would make, although that would lead them down paths ordained by us not the Lord.

All of our boys have wandered down trails we wish they would have avoided at one time or another. When they stumbled—as we all do—we had to remind each other that our sovereign Lord has paved their paths with a holy purpose.

We know our sons may fall into temptation, let sin rule in their hearts for a season, or even stray from their faith. Still, as we remember the Lord's past works, He helps us trust His plan and pace. We thank God for assuring us that nothing will snatch His people out of His hands (John 10:27–29). Even when the Israelites strayed from their loving God, He affirmed His love and pursued them. "For this is what the Sovereign LORD says: I myself will search for my sheep and look after them" (Ezekiel 34:11). As our Good Shepherd, He loves our children more than we can even begin to fathom. Though there is no guarantee that they will not reject Him or harden their hearts toward the Holy Spirit in rebellion, our loving Father doesn't want anyone to be lost. God gave us free will, which enables us to turn away from Him and run like crazy. But His ever-open arms will always be ready to offer forgiveness to every lost sheep who repents. And no one can stop God from hearing our prayers. So our most heart-deep request now is for each of our sons to develop a thriving relationship with their heavenly Father.

In the parable of the prodigal son found in Luke 15, when the youngest son demanded his inheritance, the patient father released his son without ranting over what could happen. The wild son chased worldly pleasures, squandered his finances, and compromised his honor and integrity until he hit rock bottom. He came to his senses after he lost everything, after he experienced the devastation that goes hand in hand with sinful living. Realizing his foolishness, he regretted leaving the refuge of his father's loving care and decided to go home.

Scripture doesn't mention what the father and the older son did as they waited to hear from the young son who had embraced a life of sin. The father's reaction to his younger son's return can help us paint a picture of his heart condition, though. While this wayward son was "still a long way off, his father saw him and was filled with compassion for him; he ran to his son, threw his arms around him and kissed him" (v. 20). His response to his rebellious son's return seems to be one of a father watching for his son to come on home, waiting for him with a willingness to embrace him with undeserved grace. The father didn't badger his son about his whereabouts, condemn him for his failures, or reject him. He didn't blast him with an *I-told-you-so* or guilt him with an *I-worried-about-you-every-night*.

Instead, the father rejoiced over his long-awaited return. When his son bent his head in shame, the father lifted his chin and extended mercy. It didn't matter where he'd been or what he'd done . . . he was home where he belonged, safe and loved and now equipped with a God-glorifying testimony. The father publicly proclaimed his joy over his beloved child's homecoming.

And then, just as his waiting appeared to be at an end, the father entered yet another season of waiting. As his relationship with one son was restored, he had to begin the wait for his older son's repentance.

The older brother became infuriated when he saw the whole household celebrating his brother's reappearance. His attitude reeks of resentment, bitterness, and even a bit of jealousy. "Look! All these years I've been slaving for you and never disobeyed your orders" (v. 29). Showing no compassion, he referred to his younger sibling as "this son of yours" (v. 30), severing their personal connection. As if his father's love could be earned by works, the older son seemed to think his own faithfulness over the years merited more than his brother's failings. His demands teetered between a desire for fairness rather than grace and a prideful sense of entitlement.

Our attitude during the wait reveals our heart-motives. When we live to love and serve our Father, we can be confident in knowing God is faithful, unconditionally good, and sovereign, even when we can't understand why things work out as they do. We can reflect Christlike character in and through our relationships with others, even when someone's poor choices impact us. The celebration will be extraordinary, as we trust God to nurture resilient faith in us and in the lives of those we love. We can depend on Him to keep right on working in our lives while simultaneously working in the lives of those around us. And yes, we can be forever confident that God is always loving and always ready to offer His all-sufficient grace. Knowing the Lord is working for the good of all who love Him is always something to celebrate.

INHALE

> For you make me glad by your deeds, LORD;
> I sing for joy at what your hands have done.
> How great are your works, LORD,
> how profound your thoughts!
> —PSALM 92:4–5

EXHALE

Patient Father, you are well aware of how hard it is to watch loved ones choose to stray from the security of your truth and sink into the destructiveness of self-satisfying sins.

Whether it's family members or friends, we all have people we pray will encounter your glorious and loving grace in action. We all know loved ones we hope will receive your unconditional love for them and submit every aspect of their lives to you.

We praise you now for strengthening the wandering hearts who desperately need your hope, Lord. We praise you now for the testimonies you're building when the road feels treacherous and the wait feels endless. Please forgive us for the times when we've been the ones choosing to chase sinful pleasures, when we've fallen into the rut of conforming to the world and straying from you, Good Shepherd.

Thanks for never giving up on us when we were lost. Thanks for blessing us with intercessors who prayed for us faithfully. And thanks for helping us not to give up on others. Please refresh our spirits and make our prayers bold as we place our confidence in your life-transforming truth and heart-changing love.

In Jesus's name, Amen.

- Who loved you, prayed for you, and shared the gospel with you before you surrendered your life to Christ?

- What can you do to thank them today?

- When a loved one embraces a life of sin, how can you show them love as you continue praying for their long-awaited homecoming?

- Who are you praying will receive the Lord?

- How can remembering our lives are both individually purposed and interwoven with others help you extend mercy as you wait for God to move in the lives of your loved ones?

Reliable Father,
your work in our yesterdays
strengthens our faith for today.

28

Keep Reaching

TODAY'S TRUTH

Hope keeps reaching for Jesus.

TODAY'S READING: *Mark 5:21–34*

The Lord blessed Stephanie with the perfect man in college. They attended Bible studies together and eventually planned a wonderful life as a married couple. Children? Yes. Of course, they wanted children. What a wonderful home these faithful stewards could provide for the children God had planned for them. They tried. They waited. They tried and waited. For years, they tried until doctors revealed they both had medical issues that would make it nearly impossible for them to have children. So when a friend suggested they consider foster care and adoption, Stephanie welcomed the idea that God's plan and her future family portraits might look a little bit different from her initial version of perfect.

Almost immediately after being approved for foster care, they received a middle-of-the-night call. An eight-month-old boy, severely emaciated due to malnutrition, needed an emergency placement. It didn't take long for Stephanie and her husband to file for adoption. God was answering their prayers. After four years of enduring multiple court hearings and draining bouts with the biological father, they became parents. Hallelujah!

Over time, secrets came out and their innocent baby was sentenced to a lifetime of consequences caused by his biological parents' drug abuse. Still, this child God chose for Stephanie and her husband was the answer to their years of prayer. Content with the path the Lord had paved, they continued to love their son. Soon after, God blessed them with a second adopted child. Surely, their family would be complete with this beautiful eight-day-old baby girl who desperately needed a home.

Thankful her wait was over, Stephanie invested in the lives of her two children. She'd tucked away the memories of the grief-filled nights she yearned for a biological child. Surely, she could trust her Creator had a reason to decide adoption would be her route toward motherhood. But a few months after adopting that sweet baby girl, Stephanie found out she was pregnant.

Answering their prayers in ways they never imagined possible, God had given them three children and created the perfect family *for them*. Stephanie couldn't have been more pleased . . . until their beloved first child became a man who longed to develop a relationship with his biological parents. Though she tried to support her son in the process, she felt betrayed. Wasn't she a good mother? Didn't she love him enough?

God began to prick her heart as she experienced unexpected grief, fear, anger, insecurity, and then . . . guilt. She'd asked for a child. The Lord gave her three. He'd fulfilled His promise to her, yet she still felt trapped in a seemingly endless cycle of discontent. Wanting that perfect life of her dreams distorted the joy of trusting His plan and pace are always perfect.

"The Lord helped me step out of my selfishness," she says. "I'd served my purpose in my son's life. I had to allow him to work through his stuff, so God could continue to work through mine." She asked for forgiveness and, after placing the situation back into the Lord's hands, Stephanie received a call from her son.

"I love you," he said. "You'll always be my mom. You're the one who raised me."

Stephanie realized God's plan *was* perfect, even though the journey had been harder and much more complicated than she would have liked. "The Lord helped me remember *my* promise . . . to care for the children He'd given me," she says. "God is faithful. And I'm still watching and waiting to see how He works things out."

Stephanie continues reaching for the Lord. The waiting demanded in parenting will include challenges that she may not feel prepared to handle. But having received God's promises, she trusts Him to help her walk in courage and strength. Freed from the shackles of wavering faith, Stephanie continues to reach for Jesus with confidence in His perfect love for her and her family.

Her quiet faith reminds me of another strong woman who embraced her desperate need for Jesus. Hidden in a large crowd of folks demanding Jesus's attention, a woman, waited with daring faith. Whether she had family or not, she knew the pain and loneliness of being ostracized. Her culture considered her medical condition unclean and repulsive. Afflicted with bleeding for over a decade, she understood fatigue, discouragement, and the hopelessness of a life bound by longsuffering.

According to Mark 5, this woman sought out doctors who took her money and left her worse off than before. She approached the Lord with confidence in His reputation. Reaching toward the hem of His robe, with total assurance in Jesus's abilities, the bleeding woman believed a simple touch would be enough to heal her. After a dozen years of trying, of waiting, and of being disappointed, this woman received an answer to her prayers . . . immediately. She was instantly "freed from her suffering" (v. 29). After Jesus healed the bleeding woman, He offered her much-needed assurance: "Daughter, your faith has healed you. Go in peace and be freed from your suffering" (v. 34).

Be freed? Yes. Immediately freed. Yet, she still had to choose to *live* as if she was free. Jesus seems to know that she needed more than physical healing and encouraged her to move forward in freedom.

Once God gives us a long-awaited answer to prayer, we often believe our journey is over. Why keep reaching out to Jesus when we have been given what we wanted, what we felt we needed? Why? Because our need for Him, our need for a constant connection and total dependence on Him, rises above all of the needs we can possibly experience on this side of eternity. We will never be free of our need for Jesus's touch.

Even after we've received our promise, fulfilled our dream, or experienced our healing, we can be tempted to settle for a life hindered by disbelief, fear, insecurity. We can become discontent and ungrateful. And we can even live as if we haven't received what God has already given us. We can cave into a selfishness that craves a smooth path which would nullify the need for perseverance, for trust, for faith. But when we've encountered God's freeing power and received hope through His promises, our adventure has just begun!

Hope keeps us reaching toward Jesus—the unchanging author and conductor of our faith and our waiting seasons. As we keep reaching for Jesus, we can count on Him to remain faithful and compassionate as He empowers us to walk in our inheritance as His beloved children. Once freed through *His* suffering, we can be wrapped in God's peace no matter what turmoil surrounds us. But freed of needing Jesus? Never. We may still feel hurt or disappointment, but we no longer have to be chained to the selfish discontent that distorts the joy of trusting that God's plan and pace are *always* perfect.

INHALE

Yet, the LORD longs to be gracious to you; therefore he will rise up to show you compassion. For the LORD is a God of justice. Blessed are all who wait for him!

—ISAIAH 30:18

EXHALE

Compassionate Father, thanks for reaching out to us and pursuing us with endless love. Thanks for assuring us that you are always ready to hear us and always keeping your promise to be with us.

Lord, please help us take you at your word and live in the freedom you've granted us. Give us courage and discernment to remember perseverance requires trials to refine our character.

Thanks for affirming you're within our reach at all times because you never leave us. Never. Please help us live like we believe we are your beloved children, freed from everything that hinders us from enjoying a life of peace and joy-filled faith.

In Jesus's name, Amen.

- How has God helped you accept that His plan, though different from what you expected, is perfect for you?

- Why is it often hard to live as if we're freed after we've been bound by suffering for so long?

- In what situation do you need God to help you continue reaching for Him?

Constant Comforter,
you're always within our reach
because you never let us go.

29

Wait for the Right Time

TODAY'S TRUTH

God prepares us for the moment
He decides it's time to move forward.

TODAY'S READING: *Psalm 33*

After his fortieth birthday, my husband confessed that he wanted to take a huge step toward obtaining his dream job—becoming a university professor. He longed to invest in the lives of young leaders as so many others invested in him over the years. After months of discussion and prayer, the big investment didn't make sense, the timing didn't seem right, but we both felt God nudging us forward. With unexpected peace and excitement, we decided to move ahead in this family endeavor.

Alan enrolled in a doctoral program and planned for graduation four years later. We adjusted schedules, made financial sacrifices, and prayed without ceasing as we trusted the Lord through each semester. Unexpected obstacles complicated the already rocky road and extended Alan's time in the program. Frustrated with the circumstances out of his control, he pressed onward. Seven *long* years after he started the program, our whole family traveled to Nevada for his graduation.

Overjoyed with his accomplishment, we thanked the Lord for carrying him through the long process. We prayed for God's leading and affirmed we were ready to follow Him wherever He sent us. With our list of warm-weathered preferences in hand, Alan began applying to universities, confident that the Lord would open the right door at the right time. Rejection after rejection began to chip away at his confidence. His thirty-five years in retail equipped him with great people skills, business insight, and hands-on experience with conflict management and operations. He worked hard, thanking God for a pristine record of turning around store morale and increasing profit margins. Yet he continued to receive form rejection letters from prospective employers. Did God really bring him all that way to leave his dream just out of reach?

A year passed and discouragement nipped at Alan's heels. The multiple rejections and extended pauses wore him out and nudged him toward impatience and doubt. But he believed the wait was all a part of God's perfect plan for him. He found strength in the consistency of God's character as he remained steadfast. "I wait for the LORD, my whole being waits, and in his word I put my hope" (Psalm 130:5).

Waiting while anchored in the God-breathed words of Scripture is exactly what he did. Not one, not two, but three years after graduation, Alan finally received his first interview for a position at a university . . . in Wisconsin. We packed up, left our family and friends in California, and followed God to a small Midwestern town. Not only did God bless my husband with the privilege of teaching, He also gave him the responsibility of serving as the chair of the business department. All of his experiences during the wait equipped him for the position the Lord had set aside for him.

The job isn't what he expected. It's more rewarding and much more challenging than he could have imagined. The move wasn't as easy as we would have liked, but we witnessed the Lord refining our character and strengthening our relationships with Him and others. Adjusting to our new home in our new community has often been physically and emotionally difficult.

WAITING FOR GOD

And we definitely were not excited about our first below-zero freezing day. Still, we're at peace.

Time and time again, the Lord has proven His plan and His timing are absolutely flawless. Our testimonies are riddled with reasons to praise God as He continues meeting our needs day by day. Life's big moves can be as nerve-racking as the seemingly endless waits . . . but God is the conductor who sets the tempo for both. He knows when we're truly prepared for the next step in the journey He has planned for us. With confidence in God's established faithfulness as the ultimate Promise-Keeper, we can wait for the right time, *walking* by faith and *being still* in faith.

Whatever our circumstances, whether we're filled with joy or grief, we can worship the Lord for being true to His Word and faithful to His loving character.

> By the word of the LORD the heavens were made,
>   their starry host by the breath of his mouth.
> He gathers the waters of the sea into jars;
>   he puts the deep into storehouses.
> Let all the earth fear the LORD;
>   let all the people of the world revere him.
> For he spoke, and it came to be;
>   he commanded, and it stood firm. (Psalm 33:6–9)

This is the God we serve. Hallelujah! This is the God we can trust as we praise His holy name. Hallelujah! Hallelujah! Hallelujah!

We can make our plans and even try to force them, but we can never know better than our all-knowing and all-mighty God.

> The plans of the LORD stand firm forever,
>   the purposes of his heart through all generations. (v. 11)

He sees all and considers all we do. We are powerless without our Maker and Sustainer. He watches and delivers those who place their hope in His unfailing love.

We wait in hope for the LORD;
    he is our help and our shield.
In him our hearts rejoice,
    for we trust in his holy name. (vv. 20–21)

When the weariness of waiting drags us into a pit of despair or unexpected changes cause us to quiver in our boots, God empowers us to stand firm on the foundation of His irrevocable love.

Our good, good Father refines us through the various trials and seasons of stillness. He deepens our dependence on Him and nurtures our faith in Him as He prepares us for the trek ahead. Ready and willing to follow His lead and submit to *His* heart's desire, we can surrender every aspect of our lives into His able hands with worshipful sureness. God calls us forth when He decides we've waited long enough, because only He knows how our lives are interwoven with the lives of others and when every detail is set in place according to His good and perfect will. Hemmed in by His immeasurable grace, we can remain still with a quiet assurance as we wait for the right time—which is undoubtedly God's time—to take the next step He wants us to take.

INHALE

The plans of the LORD
stand firm forever,
the purposes of his heart
through all generations.
—PSALM 33:11

EXHALE

The Great I AM, you are holy and righteous and always right on time. Thanks for being our everlasting hope. Whether we're in a holding pattern, heading into a season of transition, or hitting the brakes and taking a U-turn, please help us keep our eyes on you.

Affirm your goodness, your faithfulness, and your limitless power as we face the unknown.

Help us bask in the confidence of knowing you're always working at a steady and true pace, even when we can't see the progress we expect or desire.

Help us remain steadfast as we keep in stride with you, Lord. As we stroll through the valleys and climb the rocky ridges of life, please infuse us with overflowing gratitude for your ongoing presence.

Please give us courage to trust you're working according to your perfect will when we're tempted to push our way past your loving boundaries.

Refine our character and make us more like you as you prepare us for the wonderful works you planned to entrust to us before one of our days came to be.

As we praise you with patient and grateful hearts, help us proclaim your righteousness and follow you with bold faith. Thanks for being with us and knowing what we need in order to be who you created us to be, loving Father.

In Jesus's name, Amen.

- How has God strengthened your resolve during an extended time of waiting?

- What helps you to trust the Lord when you're facing a big move, a season of transition, or rejection?

- How does it help you to know God is working all things for the good of all who love Him, not just you or me but *all* who love Him?

In your holy name,
Lord, our hearts rejoice.

30

Waiting in Victory

TODAY'S TRUTH

Our victory is secured by the love of the Father,
the truth of the Spirit, and the power of Jesus's name.

TODAY'S READING: *John 15:26–17:26*

Annalise tucked her stark black hair behind her ear, revealing her glistening dark eyes. When I handed her the hiring packet, she smiled. Her lips quivered as she placed her trembling hand over mine. "This is my first job . . . ever," she said. "Thank you."

When Annalise walked into our church over a year before that day in the conference room, she had recently escaped an abusive marriage, completed a year of recovery from drugs, and survived eight months of homelessness with her five children. Within the first month, we celebrated her baptism. Her passion for the Lord inspired me, igniting a deeper yearning to love God as wildly as my new friend.

I smiled. "When Alan and I needed helpers for this job, we couldn't think of anyone else more trustworthy for the position."

She wiped away tears. "You won't be disappointed."

How could I be? I had the privilege of serving alongside this radiant light for Christ.

For a year, we worked side by side. Her genuine, continuous worship of God filled every room she entered. No matter what obstacles she bumped up against, no matter what losses she suffered, no matter what pain she endured, Annalise praised the Lord with authenticity. Her toothy smile could lift my spirits in an instant. Her passion for heart-to-heart chats with Jesus ignited my prayer life as I witnessed her placing every worry into God's capable hands . . . sometimes with heart-wrenching sobs of surrender or cries of grateful praise. "This will all pass," she would say when facing long waits and treacherous hikes through life's dark valleys. "Jesus is coming again. Until then, or until the day He calls me home, ain't no rocks going to praise Him on my behalf. Oh, what a glorious day it will be when we get to see Jesus face-to-face!"

When doctors diagnosed Annalise with cancer, my friend declared God's faithfulness, mercy, and power. She trusted He would care for her. She trusted He would care for her children, should He call her home before they were grown. Every Sunday she would close her eyes and sing praises to Jesus. As I watched my friend loving Jesus with all her heart, all her soul, and all her strength, I wanted to worship Him more, love Him more, believe Him more. Sometimes when the praise team played the first cords of one of our favorite worship songs, "I Can Only Imagine," we'd look at each other, smile, and worship the Lord as one.

A year later, the treatments failed and the cancer ravaged her physical body. Annalise still whispered soul-stirring prayers that always ended with a moment of vibrant praise. We prayed together as she made arrangements for her children to live with family. "I'm sad that I won't get to see my babies grow up," she said. "Still, I can hardly wait to see Jesus face-to-face!"

Annalise loved and lived for the Lord until the day He welcomed her into His loving embrace. At her standing-room-only Celebration of Life service, countless people testified how Annalise had encouraged them, prayed for them, believed in them, and even given money to help them when she was barely making ends meet. She lived for Jesus, loving Him and others with relentless joy and peace that transcended all understanding.

Every Christmas I unwrap four small ornaments that she made for me. I hang them on our tree and remember her devotion to the Lord. I rejoice over her infectious love for God and others. I thank God for creating Annalise and sharing her glorious, too-short life with me. And I pray for her now-grown children, who are trusting the Lord until they see their beautiful mama again.

As Jesus completed His earthly ministry before His arrest, He wanted to prepare His disciples for what they would face. Jesus knew each of His followers would experience a difficult life. He promised they would receive an Advocate—the Holy Spirit, the "Spirit of truth who goes out from the Father"—who would remind them who Jesus was and is and always will be (John 15:26). Jesus went on to share with His disciples—and with us—the beautiful unity of the Father, the Son, and the Holy Spirit, and our part in God's plan.

The Lord commissioned His disciples to be living testimonies of His power and grace, sharing the gospel with bold and persevering faith. He confirmed they would be misunderstood and hated, that their faith-walk would be filled with strife. He explained why He would leave them to return to the Father and why they needed to personally receive the Holy Spirit. Jesus affirmed the Spirit of truth would "prove the world to be in the wrong about sin and righteousness and judgement" (John 16:8). He declared the deception and defeat of Satan, "the prince of this world" (v. 11). The Messiah himself promised His Second Coming.

With loving patience, Jesus shared His perfect plan and comforted His disciples with the guarantee of His eternal and constant presence in the present and when He would come again. The Spirit would guide them in truth and empower them with persevering faith, as the disciples marched through the lowest valleys, trudged down the longest roads, and climbed the highest and rockiest ledges of their Meantime Mountains. They would grow weary and doubt. They would fear and want to quit. But as they recalled Jesus's promises, they would be prepared for victory.

"I have told you these things, so that *in me* you may have *peace*. In this world you *will* have trouble. But *take heart!* I *have overcome* the world" (John 16:33, emphasis mine).

Jesus equips and encourages us with His truth, affirming our need to abide in Him. He promises peace, even when we don't experience relief from our suffering on this side of eternity. Though trouble remains inevitable, we can take heart, be confident, brave, and encouraged in the face of trials and waiting seasons that feel endless and overwhelming.

Jesus—the Prince of Peace—has overcome the world and will return!

INHALE

For I am convinced that neither death nor life,
neither angels nor demons, neither the present
nor the future, nor any powers, neither height nor depth,
nor anything else in all creation, will be able to separate
us from the love of God that is in Christ Jesus our Lord.

—ROMANS 8:38–39

EXHALE

Forever faithful and loving Father, we love you. Please help us draw near to you each day.

Thanks for sending your Spirit to help us understand and obey your holy Word.

When problems worry us and cause us to dwell on the things we can't change, please shift our focus to your infallible Word and your immutable character.

Loving and living Lord Jesus, please be our strength, our hope, and our comfort today and every day. You are the reason for our everlasting joy, Abba. Help us walk and wait with confidence in your victory, with courage rooted in the work you finished on the cross. Please breathe hope into our weary spirits and refresh our souls with the guarantee of your Second Coming.

Let the sweet assurance of your Spirit's constant presence be our peace in this world, no matter what our circumstances.

We love you, mighty and merciful King of Kings and Lord of Lords. We worship you with every breath, as we inhale your truth and exhale faith-filled praises.

May your name be glorified and your power magnified in and through each day you've given us.

In Jesus's name, Amen.

- How does the promise of Jesus's Second Coming solidify our hope and comfort us with enduring peace when we face trials?

- What worries do you need to surrender to Christ today?

- What do you think about when you imagine seeing Jesus face-to-face?

God the Father,
God the Son,
God the Holy Spirit,
you secure our victory.

31
Rejuvenating Rest

TODAY'S TRUTH

*God refreshes our spirits
and empowers us to encourage others.*

TODAY'S READING: *Matthew 11:28–30*

I met Haley in the cancer center's community kitchen. When I offered her a brownie, I never expected to be rewarded with a lasting friendship with this not-yet twenty-one-year-old. I certainly didn't think God would use her to teach my forty-something self a little bit more about walking and waiting by faith.

Beautifully bald, Haley listened. She cared. And she prayed, prayed, and prayed for others. Patients and medical staff went out of their way to run into this joy-filled prayer warrior. Her badge as a cancer survivor couldn't possibly inspire half as much as the love of Christ overflowing into the lives of anyone who dared make eye contact with her.

Haley spent her time giving, giving, and giving, whether she was at the cancer care house, the clinic, or in the hospital. She spread God's love with dimpled smiles, even when her glistening eyes revealed her own pain. She presented others with handmade bracelets. I still have mine, crafted in love with colors Haley noticed I wore often.

My mom had found the overstuffed envelope taped to our door when we returned from one of her treatments at the clinic.

"You haven't even been with me for a month and you've got friends giving you presents."

I laughed. "I've been asking God to use me to encourage others and to send us support," I said, opening the construction-paper card. "We need spirit-refreshers if we're going to get through the tough days ahead of us, Mom."

Unlike me, my mother had chosen to keep to herself for the month she'd been at the clinic before my arrival. But I knew I'd need God and a friend or two reminding me to keep focused on His hope, His peace, and His presence when waiting wore me out. So I connected with the first folks I met in the elevator the day I arrived. Frank and his wife, Lori, adopted me before I unpacked my suitcase. Carrie and I became friends quickly, and it wasn't because she was an incredible baker. And God used Haley to bless me whenever I needed a breath of fresh air and a glimpse of unshakeable faith.

Knowing my need for community and intercessory prayer, given and received, I continued encouraging others and making friends until the day we left. I'm still in contact with our cancer house friends, still praying for them as they pray for me . . . as we wait to see what God has in store for our after-the-clinic days. Some are still fighting. Some are in remission. Some are processing the five-syllable punch in the gut none of us want to hear: Your cancer is back. Some, like my mom, were welcomed into the loving arms of Jesus after their long and weary fight. And some, like Haley, are still inspiring hope in others as they return to the clinic for check-ups, wait for results, process overwhelming emotions, and prepare to repeat the cycle.

The day I received Haley's package, my mom eyed my gift. "What is it?" I showed her the bracelet and read the note that promised prayers and drenched us with loving encouragement.

"Let's make her more brownies," Mom said.

Nodding, I taped the decorated paper on our card-wall, an entire wall filled with notes of encouragement and prayers sent by those who reminded us we weren't alone on this journey God had planned for us.

I slipped on the bracelet and gathered the baking supplies. "You get some rest, Mom. I'll make the treats."

"I'm not tired anymore."

Arguing was futile, so I convinced my mom to sit in a chair while I baked. We shook on it and made our way to the kitchen on the second floor. The love Haley showered on us overflowed as we worked to bless her in return. Praying for one another reminded us who God was, is, and always will be—the only One who could provide rest for our souls and carry our daily burdens today and forever.

Later, I texted Haley and her mom. They joined us in the community dining room to pray and chow down on a batch of brownies. Shortly after our dessert date, both Haley and my mom were hospitalized. I noticed nurses and patients wearing Haley's bracelets as I walked down the hallways. Although our sweet friend spent her twenty-first birthday attached to an IV in a sterile environment, nothing dimmed her infectious joy, peace, and hope in Christ. She never stopped thinking about ways to show kindness to others. When someone gave her a fancy coloring book for adults and she realized how much she enjoyed the therapeutic artistic process, she contacted the creator of the book and requested donations to share with other patients.

As Haley traveled the winding roads through the valley of waiting, Jesus remained her power source. She could pray for others, give to others, and care about others, because she made a priority of resting in the peace of God's constant presence first. Though Haley struggled with weariness at times, He revitalized her spirit so she could refresh other weary souls and nurture the genuine loving community that He'd used to lift her up in love.

Jesus gives us the same recipe for peace-filled waiting in Matthew 11:28–30. The Lord beckons His disciples to draw close to Him when we're feeling beat and burdened. He knows waiting requires both rest and hard work. Jesus *will* give us breathers when we answer His invitation to take that first step toward Him, even when that step toward surrender comes after a bout with stubbornness.

"Take my yoke upon you and learn from me, for I am gentle and humble in heart, and you will find rest for your souls. For my yoke is easy and my burden is light" (Matthew 11:29–30). The Lord's load is light because He is limitless in power. When we take on His yoke, we're like toddlers helping a parent with luggage. Our good Father allows us to hold the handle as He lifts the brunt of the weight.

During His earthly ministry, Jesus taught the value of relying on the Father and resting our souls. Jesus, fully Man and fully God, spent time with the Father in stillness and prayer, restored in peace and replenished so He could continue giving of himself. When His flesh weakened, His Spirit rose in strength.

We too can experience the wonder of being revived in the presence of our boundless and bountiful God. Leaning into God's restoring peace and resting in His mercy, we can rely on His might not our own. We can reserve our strength by allowing the Lord to *be* our strength. We can sleep because God never sleeps. We can give because we can't out-give God. As the Lord rejuvenates us through the peace of His ongoing presence, His power and love overflow in our hearts and into the lives of others. Like He did for Haley, He will refresh our spirits and use us to encourage others as we're encouraged through every second He ordains for our well-purposed wait.

INHALE

Come to me, all you
who are weary and burdened,
and I will give you rest.
—MATTHEW 11:28

EXHALE

Everlasting God, thanks for energizing us with confidence in your eternal hope and abounding love. Please shine the vibrant light of your infallible truth onto our current situation. Help us surrender to you, to be confident that you are our strength.

Help us trust your guidance, no matter what obstacles we face during the wait. Transform us with your flawless holy-breathed words of Scripture as we open ourselves up to be your vessels of truth-sharing hope during the wait.

Thanks for shielding us, sustaining us, and fighting on our behalf as you affirm you are the One True God. You are our Rock, our Refuge, and the good, good Shepherd who secures our footing on the paths you've chosen for us.

Help us rise up with joyful expectation and resilient faith through every moment you've purposed for your glory as we receive and share your overflowing love.

In Jesus's name, Amen.

- How can giving to others and sharing what God has done in our lives rejuvenate our faith when we're overwhelmed with burdens or just plain tired of waiting?

- How has God strengthened you during a long wait or an extended trial?

- In what situation do you need to be refreshed by the love of Christ?

- Who can you shower with God's overflowing love today?

Almighty God, anchor our hope in your limitless power, your constant presence, and your faith-strengthening love.

Conclusion

Waiting Expectantly

I am a part of something so much bigger than my own small sphere of influence. You are a part of something so much bigger than your small sphere of influence. As God's children, who submit to His authority and trust daily in His perfect plan and pace, we will always be in waiting. But we're waiting for so much more than "just" relief, an answer to prayer, miraculous provision, or an obstacle-moving event. Like the persevering people in the Hall of Faith (Hebrews 11), we're waiting for the fulfillment of God's promise through His Son, our Lord and Savior Jesus Christ.

The heavyweights of God-worshippers in Hebrews 11

> were all commended for their faith, yet none of them received what had been promised, since God had planned something better for us *so that* only together *with us* would they be made perfect. *Therefore*, since we are surrounded by such a great cloud of witnesses, let us throw off everything that hinders and the sin that so easily entangles. And *let us run with perseverance* the race marked out for us, *fixing our eyes on Jesus*, the pioneer and perfecter of faith. *For the joy set before him* he endured the cross, scorning its shame, and sat down at the right hand of the throne of God. *Consider him* who endured such opposition from sinners, *so that* you will not grow weary and lose heart. (Hebrews 11:39–12:3, emphasis mine)

Our faith-journeys are intertwined with those who came before us, those who walk with us, and those who have yet to believe. We can run and rest with perseverance, confident that our all-knowing God paved the perfect road He's planned to walk with us. As we abide in Christ, we can soak in His soothing words of infallible truth. The Lord himself will empower us to rejoice in the "joy set before" Him—the same promise we receive when we surrender our lives to Christ, repent of our sins, and receive the Holy Spirit—eternity with the Father.

Consider all that our Lord Jesus endured for us, all He suffered for us, all He gave up when He put on flesh and became fully man and fully God, the High Priest who understands us completely. When we consider Him, our flesh may grow weary. But when we abide in Him, our spirits will rise up in victorious praise and never, ever, ever lose heart and give up.

As we worship Jesus until He comes again or calls us home, we are waiting for God.

Our wait is never in vain. What we learn in the wait is never useless. No matter how hard the road, how difficult the travel arrangements, or how long the deliberate delays He's carved out for us, we can count on God to be our strength, our peace, and our eternal hope.

Jesus will come again. Hallelujah! Hallelujah! Hallelujah!

Until then, we can exalt our Lord Jesus with a lifestyle of worship, trusting daily in His plan and pace as we wait expectantly for His promised return.

Praise the LORD.

Praise God in his sanctuary;
    praise him in his mighty heavens.
Praise him for his acts of power;
    praise him for his surpassing greatness.

Praise him with the sounding of the trumpet,
    praise him with the harp and lyre,
praise him with timbrel and dancing,
    praise him with the strings and pipe,
praise him with the clash of cymbals,
    praise him with resounding cymbals.

Let everything that has breath praise the LORD.

Praise the LORD.

—PSALM 150

Acknowledgments

I thank God for the pleasure and privilege of sharing His truth and love to the ends of the earth through writing and speaking. The Holy Spirit always supplies all I need in order to do all He places before me. And my daily battle with chronic pain and fatigue reminds me that I can't do anything without Him or the loving folks He uses to equip and encourage me as we trust daily in His plan and pace.

My husband, Dr. W. Alan Dixon, Sr. and our son, Xavier, trust me to write about how God works in and through our lives. Their ongoing support is priceless. I'm thankful for my stepson, A.J., who cheers me on (as long as I keep him out of my stories), for friends who feel like family and make me laugh, especially Juanita (Nee-Nee) Johnson, Cendy Trujillo, and Jennifer Thomas, and for my darlin' dogs, Jazzy and Callie, who supply cuddles and comic relief as I write.

I'm grateful for every courageous faith-warrior who allowed me to share a snippet of their story in *Waiting for God*, for my Credo Communications agents, Timothy J. Beals and Karen Neumair, and for every single person in the Discovery House family (from preparation to printing to packing), especially Dawn Anderson, Miranda Gardner, Cathy Sall, Meaghan Minkus, and Emily Van Houten.

God surrounds me with incredible prayer support: Colleen Shine Phillips, Jen Lindsay, Rachel Dodge, the Fabulous Five

(Julie Williams, Kathy Ide, Sandy Barela, Susan Beatty, and Sami Abrams), and my Praying Peeps on Facebook and Instagram.

The talented authors and editors who serve with me through the ministry of *Our Daily Bread* continue to inspire and help me grow. Special thanks to Joyce Dinkins, Andy Rogers, Anne Cetas, and Tim Gustafson. Faithful spiritual mentors have invested in me as God nurtured my deep love of studying and teaching the Bible: Pastor Bob Lawler, Ms. Virginia Moody, Barbara Pfahlert, and our FBC family. Gifted writers have encouraged me and taught me how to develop my craft as a tool for ministry: Sandra Byrd, Shelly Beach, Francine Rivers, Steve Laube, Susan King, Wendy Lawton, Susy Flory, Janet McHenry, Patricia Raybon, Jan Kern, Kay Strom, and many others who have served at the Mount Hermon, Oregon, and SoCal Christian Writers conferences.

Thanks to all who have endorsed *Waiting for God* and are helping me spread the word, especially my dedicated launch team, the Celebrate Lit marketing and promoting masters (Sandy and Denise Barela), and my new Fondy Friends (special shout-out to Carmen Leal, Susan Baganz, and our Community Church family).

Joy overflows as I thank God for the people He's used to love me, help me grow spiritually, and bless my writing journey, and for the doctors and their staff members who help me continue serving the Lord through the wait (especially Dr. Gomez, Dr. Choi, Dr. Anand, and Dr. Rao). I'm grateful for the pleasure and privilege of serving and praying for every reader the Lord leads my way, particularly those in my blog family and my Facebook, Twitter, and Instagram fam. To God be the glory, the honor, and the praise, praise, praise!

Help us get the word out!

Our Daily Bread Publishing exists to feed the soul with the Word of God.

If you appreciated this book, please let others know.

- Pick up another copy to give as a gift.

- Share a link to the book or mention it on social media.

- Write a review on your blog, on a bookseller's website, or at our own site (ourdailybreadpublishing.org).

- Recommend this book for your church, book club, or small group.

Connect with us:

 @ourdailybread

 @ourdailybread

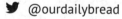 @ourdailybread

Our Daily Bread Publishing
PO Box 3566
Grand Rapids, Michigan 49501 USA

 books@odb.org